Praise for *Cra*

"In a humorous but powerful way, Bil asks hard questions and deconstructs Christianity's hiccups but also provides new solutions for the church and individuals going forward. As I work at reconstructing a new path forward free of unhelpful dogma and a theistic notion of God, I am encouraged by Bil's ideas in reframing the practice of prayer and biblical interpretation."
  —Megan Dukett, Program Manager of Education and Interpretive Services, Mission San Juan Capistrano

"*Cramming for the Finals* is the best explanation of progressive Christianity I have seen. I look forward to leading courses using this book."
  —Jacquelyn Marshall, author and Christian education instructor

"For readers looking to explore their own connection to faith, here is a fascinating account of an Episcopal priest who is not afraid to delve deep and ask faith-challenging questions. He invites readers along to open up and expand their thinking about the church, scripture, doctrine, a theistic god, and a divine Jesus."
  —Rev. Dr. Paul Tellström, Senior Pastor, Irvine United Congregational Church

"I have questioned some of the biblical stories since I was a child, so it is refreshing to find a book that gives answers. At times I have felt I was alone on my faith journey, but *Cramming for the Finals* lets me know that I am not."
  —Carol Getz, educator

"This is a challenging and provocative book that encourages discussion to facilitate a deeper understanding of one's faith. I highly recommend reading it with an open mind and heart and trying on the ideas the book presents. If all people practiced 'God is love' theology, the world would be a better place."

—Tamra Goris, artist, mother of two teenagers, and progressive Episcopalian

Cramming for the Finals is a challenge to my present personal faith. As an encouragement for readers to examine their own faith journey, giving it 21st-century theological relevance, Dr. Aulenbach shares his personal nonclerical and clerical story. What is important today, he says, is how we do life, how we daily live life to its fullest. The Creation (God) and agape (Matt. 25:40) are key!"

—Rev. Canon Franklin S. H. Chun, Bishop's Chaplain to Retired Clergy, The Episcopal Diocese of Hawai'i

"Aulenbach weaves humor into his narrative about religious beliefs, scriptures, what lies beyond this life, and the nature of God's existence. Some might regard parts of the text as irreverent, but a careful reading will reveal the author's lifetime of study and thought about human belief systems."

—Steve Goetz, retired faculty, Orange Coast College

"In my late eighties, I find myself searching for the experience of God in a scientific world. *Cramming for the Finals* is a road map for my own personal spiritual journey and also contains exciting ideas for the future of the institutional church."

—Joan Thompson, MA, retired Senior Center Director

Cramming for the Finals

WILLIAM AULENBACH, MDIV, MSW, PHD

Summit Run Press

Summit Run Press
360 E. First Street, #451
Tustin, CA 92780
www.summitrunpress.com

Ordering Information
Quantity sales. Special discounts are available on quantity purchases by corporations, associations, and others. For details, contact the "Special Sales Department" at the address above.

Orders by US trade bookstores and wholesalers. Please contact BCH: (800) 431-1579 or visit www.bookch.com for details.

"Leaving Home" is reprinted with permission of David Keighley.

Printed in the United States of America

Aulenbach, William, author.
    Cramming for the finals : new ways of looking at old
    church ideas / William Aulenbach. -- First edition.
        pages cm
    Includes bibliographical references and index.
    LCCN 2017903289
    ISBN 978-0-9987689-3-9 (pbk.)
    ISBN 978-0-9987689-4-6 (ebook)

    1. Christianity--21st century. 2. Church history.
    3. Theology, Doctrinal--Popular works. 4. Postmodernism
    --Religious aspects--Christianity. 5. Aulenbach,
    William.   I. Title.

BR121.3.A95 2017   270.8'3
QBI17-900049

First Edition

21 20 19 18 17   10 9 8 7 6 5 4 3 2 1

Dedicated to Father Tom Schutter, a wonderful friend and progressive Roman Catholic priest from St. Luke's Parish, Carol Stream, Illinois.

In honor of Brad Allen, a fellow marine, a classmate in seminary, and my best friend, who was killed instantly in a motorcycle accident in October 1958. Brad is still teaching me life's lessons.

Contents

Preface

Shalom Bienvenida Welcome Bienvenue.

Why the book title?

Two little boys, about ten, were playing, running in and out of the house. In the corner by a window was an old woman, rocking in her rocking chair with a Bible in her lap. Occasionally she would read a little and then doze off. She'd wake up, read some more, and then doze off again. No one seemed to pay much attention to her, and she never said a word. Finally, the little boy visiting asked his friend, "Who's that old lady in the corner reading the Bible?" Without batting an eyelash, his friend answered, "Oh, she's my grandma. She's cramming for the finals!"

This is a fun story! It has received laughs for years.

But I don't believe it for a second. As far as I am concerned, there are no "finals." And I have no idea what's next, if anything.

Here's what Genesis 3:19 states: "You are dust and to dust you shall return."

What is really important to me is how we do life today and that I have a guru who has shown me the way to lead my life to the fullest.

So this book is my rather novel, fun, exciting, interesting way of "Cramming for the Finals." It's taken me almost eighty-five years to figure it out.

Acknowledgments

I write my books primarily for laity. I am not a scholar or an academic, and I am not recognized as any sort of authority. I simply want to present different ideas to those folks who want to have their minds stretched a bit.

With that in mind, I asked a group of people whom I admire to look at my book and give me honest feedback. I call them my focus group. We met three times and discussed what I had presented. The group was outstanding and I can't thank them enough for helping me change direction, eliminate a ton of unimportant material, and sharpen the content.

Anne Aulenbach, my wife of fifty-five years, who always claims she will be very quiet in a meeting and then offers great suggestions. I love the fact that we are still best friends. I am one lucky guy!

Cristina Calderon, a good friend from a previous parish. She did a great job of getting the book ready for my focus group.

John Emerson, a very humble man with a great smile who has an uncanny ability to speak truth in a quiet, loving way. His input took me in a whole different direction.

Shirley Lorenz, whose tough love and sincere honesty is a breath of fresh air and right on.

Don Mansell, a recovering Roman Catholic whose favorite brain game seems to be to question everything. He is very good at it.

Susan Sayre, an attorney and a courageous woman who loves to serve the hurting world.

Tamra Goris, whom I have known as a friend since she was nineteen, almost thirty-five years ago. She's articulate and progressive and has given me great ideas about this book.

The following people were not part of the focus group but contributed in other ways.

The Reverend Ken Wyant, a retired United Church of Christ pastor, biblical scholar, and member of Irvine United Congregational Church (IUCC), and the Reverend Dr. George Johnson, a retired Evangelical Lutheran Church in America pastor, lecturer, and member of IUCC, who both evaluated my book.

Sharon Goldinger, my longtime friend, editor, and wonderful taskmaster.

I also need to mention two other people who have been a big influence on me.

Father Tom Schutter, a very popular Roman Catholic priest whose large, fun parish was located in Carol Stream, Illinois. Tom died of a massive heart attack as he vested for mass on Saturday, April 2, 2011. On the way home from the celebration of his life, I told Annie that I wanted to write this book. I think he would have liked it.

Brad Allen, a fellow Marine Corps officer, PK (preacher's kid), and student at the Church Divinity School of the Pacific, Berkeley, California. Brad was killed in a horrendous motorcycle accident in October 1958. I survived, but Brad has been teaching me life's lessons ever since.

What a lucky person I am to have such wonderful people guiding me as I try to help others look at their faith journey and keep a first-century prophetic sage relevant in the twenty-first century.

Proceed with Caution

I f you're looking for a book to challenge your thinking, want to see heresy in action, are interested in finding a definition of *Christ* that works for you, or are curious about the thoughts of an eighty-five-year-old Episcopal priest who has gone through hell and back, then this book may interest you—especially the part where a fire engine broadsides him on his motorcycle.

However, if you don't want anyone to mess with your thinking, refuse to disagree with what your church tells you, long to live in the fourth century, believe that NoOneUpThere wrote the Bible and that Jesus rose from the dead, this book could be dangerous— but I'd still love for you to read it.

When I went to seminary almost sixty years ago, most of the ideas in this book were not even ideas yet. I was not aware of new, exciting approaches to studying God, Jesus, Paul, or the newly found eighteen gospels. In this book, I want to give you a bird's-eye view of how much has drastically changed over the past six decades. In my seminary days, we learned that Paul wrote fourteen of the letters in the New Testament. Today we know he wrote only seven of them. In 1957, we studied only the four gospels instead of the twenty-two we know of now, and the idea of a historical Jesus didn't exist.

I begin this book with my unusual faith journey from child-hood to my ninth decade. I then offer a unique and controversial perspective on twenty church-related subjects and introduce you to a bunch of Jesuses, including the real one, who packs an earthshak-ing message that sometimes gets lost in all the felonious dogma and doctrine of the church. I suggest that the birth narrative and resurrection are powerful metaphors and discuss how we should prepare for death. Finally, I share some ideas about how to mend the institutional church, which I see as broken.

Bil's Dictionary

Every person has his or her own vocabulary. Here's mine, so you can better understand my story.

agape: The Greek word for the highest form of love. Agape is unconditional and totally accepting of everyone. Chapter 5 goes into some detail on this subject.

Annie: The woman to whom I have been married since June 17, 1961. She gave birth to our three daughters, Gretchen (54), Heidi (52), and Alison (50), and is still my best friend who enjoys doing everything with me except watching sports and *Lockup* on television. She likes to be called Anne, but after all these years, she is Annie to me.

apostle: One who is sent. (See also *disciple*.)

Brad Allen: A very important friend whom you will meet and get to know throughout my book.

Dead Sea Scrolls: Ancient Jewish writings discovered in 1947 in a cave near the Dead Sea and thought to be written by the Essenes (an apocalyptic group that existed at the time of Jesus). They are sometimes confused with the Nag Hammadi Library, ancient Gnostic writings that were discovered in 1945 by a Bedouin in the Egyptian village of Nag Hammadi.

disciple: One who is taught. (See also *apostle*.)

Docetism: One who believes that Jesus appeared human but was really God and only pretended that the nails in his hands and feet hurt.

Father Tom Schutter: A man to whom this book was dedicated. Tom became a close friend when I heard that he was using my books to teach some of his classes. He was very progressive, loved Bishop John Spong's material, and was a true pastor. I was honored to be one of the three speakers at his "Celebration of Life" service, attended by over two thousand people. On the way home from that celebration, I told Annie that I needed to write a book honoring him. Here it is.

fundamentalist: One who reads the Bible literally, loves the book of Revelation, preaches fire-and-brimstone sermons, and uses lots of threats.

Gnostic: Pertaining to the belief that the divine had become wrapped up in evil forces and the only way to understand it was by acquiring secret knowledge (gnosis).

Hellenism: The spread of Greek culture and language throughout the Mediterranean, starting around the time of Alexander the Great, that heavily influenced the early church.

IUCC: Irvine United Congregational Church, which welcomes all people regardless of where they are on their life's journey, reaches out to hurting folks all over the world, provides trained listeners to help anyone going through life's challenges, and openly discusses everything. IUCC even lets me hang around. I bet Jesus would like IUCC. (See also *Open and Affirming*.)

Jesus Seminar: A group within the Westar Institute of two hundred-plus scholars, called fellows, from all over the world who meet regularly to discuss all aspects of religion from a scholarly point of view. The seminar was started in 1985 by Robert Funk and other prominent scholars. I am a huge fan, read the group's materials, attend some of their conferences, and find them a breath of fresh air in an antiquated system.

Jewish Jesus: Jesus was a Jew his whole life. He did not start the Christian church and would have had no idea what the word *Christian* meant. All his early Followers were Jewish, as was Paul. I repeat this ad nauseam in my books because too many still believe Jesus was Christian.

Lake of Galilee: Also known as the Sea of Galilee, Lake of Gennesaret (or Geneseret), Lake of Chinnereth, Lake of Tiberias, Lake of Tabariyeh, or Lake of Tarichaea. A lake in northern Palestine that is thirteen miles long and eight miles wide. It has now been fished out, but in its heyday, it was very important to the Romans, the Herodians, and Jesus.

Messiah: Hebrew word meaning "the anointed one." In Greek, it's *Christos*, from which we have gotten the word *Christ*. (*Christ* is not Jesus's last name, but some people use it as a cuss word.)

midrash: In Judaism, the art of interpreting the written as well as the oral Torah. To understand the deeper meaning of the New Testament gospels, one must use the art of midrash.

Nag Hammadi Library: A collection of about fifty texts discovered in 1945 by a Bedouin in the Egyptian village of Nag Hammadi. These writings are sometimes confused with the Dead Sea Scrolls.

NoOneUpThere: My term for a theistic god who doesn't exist, especially in the twenty-first century, when most people know better but won't admit it. When we get rid of NoOneUpThere, the message of Jesus starts to make even greater sense.

Open and Affirming (or O&A): A designation given to churches, institutions, and synagogues that accept all people wherever they are on life's journey. Unfortunately, most churches have lists, some very long, of those who aren't acceptable in their club. Lists are the work of the devil, who doesn't exist.

rector: In the Anglican Communion, the person in charge of a church, hired by a vestry or board of directors, who has a great deal of authority—too much, in my opinion.

St. Mattress: A very popular church where one doesn't even have to get out of bed to attend. Some folks call it St. Sack's.

Sunday school theology: A belief that goes something like this: God is a white man who lives up in heaven, runs the world, judges all and then sends them to hell, wrote the King James English Bible, sent his only son down to be murdered for you, listens to and answers prayers, and hates sex. His son is divine and white, started Christianity, was the first Christian, performed unbelievable miracles, started the church, wrote *The Book of Common Prayer*, and then ascended like a rocket to heaven (he is still orbiting) and sent down a ghost. His last name is Christ, and he disapproves of those who are not heterosexual or anyone who isn't perfect. Sound familiar?

Torah: A Hebrew word meaning "guidance or direction" that later became the basis for Jewish law, or the Law of God as given to Moses. It includes the first five books of the Old Testament: Genesis, Exodus, Leviticus, Numbers, and Deuteronomy.

Westar Institute: See *Jesus Seminar*.

Wisdom comes with age. But sometimes age comes alone.
—Unknown

PART I

CRAMMING FOR THE FINALS

CHAPTER 1

My Unique Faith Journey

Honesty and frankness make you vulnerable.
Be honest and frank anyway.
—Kent M. Keith, "Anyway: The Paradoxical Commandments"

I suspect all people feel their life journey and faith journey is unique because every human being is unique. There can be no "one size fits all." My faith journey explains where I am today—a long way from where I started this journey on October 28, 1932.

I was born in Detroit, the second child and only son of an Episcopal clergyman and a schoolteacher. I was baptized when I was three weeks old, whether I wanted to be or not. I can't remember a thing about it. My mother said I was a good kid. When I was four, our family moved to Philadelphia, where my father had accepted the position of rector at a dying church that needed a resurrection.

My father was a flamboyant, outspoken, controversial clergyman who packed his church every Sunday. He was my childhood hero, and as much as I wanted to emulate him, I was totally overwhelmed by the idea of preaching two or three sermons weekly. One of my favorite childhood games was "church," where I was the minister, usually doing some serious preaching to a nonexistent congregation.

The Church

Dad's church was the most important part of my childhood and adolescent life. However, Sunday school was so boring that I dropped out at eleven years old. In the sixth grade I was sent to a private Episcopal boys' day school because I was not doing much in my predominantly black public school.

The new school, the Episcopal Academy, had chapel every day and sacred studies once a week, both of which I found extremely boring except when Dad spoke in chapel. He upset everything, but the students loved him. Most of the other speakers were snoozers. I was a flop at everything at prep school except going to Saturday detention, at which I excelled because of my big mouth and "forgetting" to do all my homework. In 1950, I barely graduated from prep school, ranking fifty-fifth out of a class of fifty-seven.

Church, not school, was the center of my life. I loved Christ Church and St. Michael's in Germantown, Philadelphia, Pennsylvania. I was an acolyte—a youth group participant and leader, a gofer for Dad, and a helper to anyone who needed assistance. When I was fourteen I was awarded a special cross for my devotion and loyalty to the church.

My Wake-Up Call

After high school I went to Kenyon College, in Gambier, Ohio, founded by an Episcopal bishop in 1824. It was an all-men's school then with less than five hundred students. My higher education started slow. Studying got in the way of partying, and I almost flunked out at the end of the first semester of my sophomore year. The Korean War was heating up at that time, and draft boards where looking for my kind. They needed gun fodder.

That caught my attention very quickly, especially after a disastrous party weekend and the dean's alerting me that I had three Fs and a D going into finals, six weeks away. That sobered me up. I had to choose: buckle down or be gun fodder. I buckled down that afternoon—truly buckled down.

Long story short, six weeks later I managed to eke out three Cs and one D, and the dean was impressed. He never thought I could do it. This was a great wake-up call.

I then became rather successful at college—in academics, on the sports field, and in leadership roles. However, my faith took a nosedive. Chapel was boring, the Bible was packed with lies, only weaklings went to church and I didn't need it—or so I thought. So I said bye-bye to God, Jesus, the Holy Ghost, and church and hello to the Marine Corps.

I Found Religion Again—in the Marines

I had no idea what I wanted to do after college, and going into the ministry was way, way in the back of my mind. My lacrosse coach, a highly decorated World War II vet, convinced me that joining the Corps would be a good way to mature and learn new life skills. I heeded his advice and received more that I had bargained for. I had a "reconversion" experience.

In my first week of boot camp, I was drilling the platoon I was in and forgot a command, which resulted in my marching the forty-four men into a chain-link fence. Once the platoon sergeant had pulled the platoon out and lined up the men, he approached me, nose to nose, and said, "Aulenbach, you ain't got no more brains than an ant!" I thought that expression was very funny and laughed.

Bad idea! The drill sergeant thought I was laughing *at* him, not *with* him, and thereafter he made my life miserable every day for the twelve weeks of boot camp. Every Friday he would flunk me out of officer training and on Saturday the review committee would send me back to his platoon. When we had only a week to go, Sarge flunked me out one more time. Ten of us misfits spent five grueling days with five heavily decorated World War II officers who were our officers review team. We were tested in every way.

The night before "D(ecision) day" I went to the slop chute (enlisted men's club) before I hit the sack. Walking home, I saw the chapel, went in, and sat in a pew. Suddenly I had this unbelievable calming that suggested, "Whatever happens, you have your faith and the tools to make anything work for good." No voices, images, or hocus-pocus—just peace. That night I slept like a baby.

The next day, I realized that I had thrown the baby (God, Jesus) out with the bathwater (the church). Bad mistake! In the morning, I stood before the members of the review team. They were tough on me and made the decision that I would not be commissioned and would spend the next two years as Private Aulenbach. Oh well. I knew that I had the tools to make "Private" work.

When I went into an office to get my new orders to be a private, the phone rang. The corporal who answered it said, "Are you Aulenbach? Return immediately to the review team."

I hurried back to the room, wondering why I was called back. I was invited in and told, "Aulenbach, you have followed your orders exactly as commanded. You will be commissioned a second lieutenant tomorrow." It was a good day for me and my faith.

Officers School went well. When I graduated, I was given orders to report to Camp Pendleton in California. From there I received orders to go to Hawai'i, not Korea, to be a tank officer at Kaneohe Marine Corps Air Base.

My Unusual Call to the Ministry

In the Marines, I never missed a Sunday of church unless I was on maneuvers. I went to a little Episcopal church where I met my friend Brad Allen.

I had a great time being a marine, traveling all over the Pacific basin. At one Marine Corps function, I met the Episcopal Bishop of Hawai'i. He invited me to lunch, where he asked me about my going into the ministry. I confessed that it was way in the back of my mind. He then said, "If you ever decide to give it a try, I'm happy to help you."

Although I enjoyed being a marine and seemed to be reasonably successful at it, I had a feeling deep down inside that this was not what I wanted to do with the rest of my life. I was much more interested in helping people than killing them.

Then it happened—I had my calling. I was the executive officer of a motor-transport outfit at the time, and our base was scheduled for an inspection by inspectors general from Marine Corps headquarters in Washington, DC. The inspector arrived two hours early, catching my troops in the middle of preparing the vehicles, facilities, and themselves. Obviously, we did not look at all like the squared-away outfit we were. Even though the inspector seemed to understand that there must have been a scheduling mistake, he immediately went to the battalion colonel and told him what a mess my outfit was. The colonel chewed me out for a situation that was beyond my control. All of a sudden, I had a powerful feeling that I needed to be in seminary.

When the colonel finished his tirade, I told him that when I left his office, I was going to make a phone call to get out of the Marines and go to seminary. He couldn't believe I had the nerve to tell him that—and neither could I. I called the bishop and said, "Bishop, I just had my calling to go to seminary." I told him the story. The bishop, who had been in Hawai'i since 1941, knew every high-ranking officer in all branches of the military in the islands. He must have immediately called a Marine Corps bigwig because within ten days I had orders to report to Terminal Island, San Francisco, and be discharged. The bishop also called the Church Divinity School of the Pacific in Berkeley, and I was accepted as a junior (a first-year student in seminary) for the fall semester.

On the first day of seminary, much to my great surprise, there was my Marine Corps buddy Brad.

When classes began, the first thing the professors did was rip apart all our Sunday school theology and start to lay a new and more solid foundation. At first, it was a bit frightening. My head was being crammed with new knowledge and ideas, and I loved the experience. I knew my life was changing for the better. I felt that I had found a stable rudder on the ship of life. I just had to learn how to use it in my daily living. That was going to take time.

My Motorcycle

In my second year of seminary, life couldn't have been more exciting. But I was not prepared for how radically my reality was about to change.

On a beautiful Friday afternoon in October, Brad and I hopped on our motorcycles to go to Tilden Park, above Berkeley. About two blocks from the seminary, a fire truck answering a call for a brush fire hit us both broadside. Brad was killed instantly, and I ended up with a badly broken lower right leg and all sorts of other relatively minor injuries.

Although my own injuries and Brad's death altered the course of my life, one of the biggest theological bombs happened the next day when a professor-priest from the seminary came to pay me a visit. He was an internationally known prayer tycoon—a strange man, aloof, mysterious, and in my humble opinion, not authentic. He even admitted to praying for over three thousand people a day by quickly flipping through a Rolodex while saying a "cover-all-bases" prayer. I found this very strange—still do.

When this priest visited me, I was really groggy—my right leg up in sling, a huge bandage on my right thigh where the brake handle had dug in and ripped out a chunk of flesh, my right hand in a cast—and he said to me, *"You and Brad must have done something terrible to deserve this."*

I couldn't believe it. His words were like another fire truck running me over, but I had enough presence of mind to order him out of the room and tell him to never come back. I didn't want anything to do with a god who would kill an outstanding man like

Brad. I came to the conclusion that such a god does not exist. I was then faced with the challenge of figuring out who God is.

My accident led to several other life-changing experiences. The first had to do with my stay at the hospital. The doctors told me I would have to be in a hospital bed for two months, which meant I would lose my GI Bill of Rights benefits and have to drop out of seminary with no place to live, no work, no money, and a rather nebulous future. But when another Episcopal priest came to visit me, I shared my dilemma. He asked me how long I wanted to stay. I said, "One week." He replied that 90 percent of healing takes place in the mind with positive, creative thinking. I really liked that concept.

When my orthopedic physician came into my room later that afternoon, I told him that I could stay only a week. He said, "There's no way you can leave here in a week," and reminded me that he could never consider discharging me until I was eating and all my systems were working. Ugh! Who likes hospital food?

Some friends from seminary came to visit me and agreed to help by bringing me appetizing food. They returned later that evening with a small tenderloin steak, peas, and mashed potatoes along with a small jar labeled "apple jelly." I thought that was weird until I discovered it was filled with white wine. They continued providing these dinners with apple jelly for the next few nights. The doctor noticed that my condition was improving and told me that he'd consider letting me leave once I mastered crutches and promised to visit his office every day.

I quickly learned to walk with crutches and was released from the hospital after ten days. I became a firm believer that 90 percent of all healing is in our heads. I also realized that life, on a daily basis, is terminal, so I had better live it to the fullest.

The second life-changing experience after my accident happened when it was time to remove my leg cast almost nine months after the accident. The doctor took off the cast, but my leg was as thin as a pencil and not ready to be walked on. So, after a few days, my leg went back into the cast for another three months, which meant that I would have to stay in Berkeley for the summer. That sounded boring until one of my professors suggested doing a study entitled "The Old Testament's Influence on the Gospels." It was a fascinating study and would prove to be a game-changer in my life. Then to help add to a great summer, I made trips to the wine country, went to Seals Stadium to watch Willie Mays, and had fun with a UC Berkeley coed.

To graduate from seminary and to be ordained, I, like every student, had to take two sets of examinations: one administered by the seminary to see if I had been properly brainwashed in the Episcopal tradition and the other administered by my diocese to see if I was ready to be ordained. I did well on both exams because I had learned that I needed to tell examiners want they wanted to hear, not what I truly believed. Had I shared my true beliefs with them, I suspect that I never would have graduated or been ordained. Unfortunately, this attitude keeps the institutional church stagnant.

I had reservations about some of the dogma and doctrine to which I was committing, but I attributed them to my youth and thought that as I aged in the ministry, my questions would all fall into place. Not true! They became bigger.

Another Life-Changing Experience

After I graduated and was ordained, I spent the summer of 1960 in Europe discovering "history" and coeds. When I arrived in Rome, I wanted to see Pope John XXIII, a hero of mine. He was bringing the Roman Catholic church into the twentieth century with his forward-thinking message of unity across denominations. I found a phone number for the papal office (it was very easy to do back in 1960), called it, and explained that I was an American Episcopal pastor who greatly admired the pope. The receptionist told me, in English, that the pope was at the summer palace, Castle Gondolfa, about eighty kilometers outside of Rome. However, she would be happy to give me a letter allowing me to have an audience with the pope along with a small number of other visitors. I jumped at the opportunity, picked up my ticket, and drove to the Castle.

I can still see and feel the presence of holiness as John XXIII came into the room, carried on a pallet on the shoulders of four men. Some one hundred other folks were gathered. People started clapping, whistling, and cheering as John went around the room greeting people. He blessed a clergy collar I had, and I was able to take this "holiness" back home with me.

Although I was still a neophyte in the clergy business, I felt that what was happening in Christianity was the coming of the Kingdom of God, on earth. Churches were being built. People filled them. Christians were talking with each other and learning to work together. Biblical criticism was encouraged in progressive seminaries and churches. Seminaries were full of men (no women yet) who were eager to help bring on the Kingdom. Liturgies were translated into the vernacular, women were being considered for ordination, and churches and clergy had a great deal of influence on society and politics. I was excited to be part of the church's future.

The Church—with Pay

When I began my ministry in Hawai'i, my first assignment was to serve as assistant rector in a large, affluent suburban parish. My main job was to guide 350 teenagers who belonged to that congregation, and I was eager to get on with my life's work.

The first rector I worked under, John Morrett, was a very spiritual man who had lived through the Bataan Death March and Japanese concentration camps, which he attributed to his deep faith. He was a great teacher on how to be a pastor, even though he sent me to the bishop after my first sermon because he perceived it as erroneous theology. The bishop sided with me, but he made me promise not to tell the rector. I had been on the job for only three weeks and already I was in trouble, a pattern often repeated.

Most clergy coming out of seminary are assigned youth work and consider it a form of torture that one must go through if one is going to learn to be a clergyman or advance in the church hierarchy. It was hard to find an Episcopal clergyperson who really enjoyed it.

I loved it and had a tremendous experience. One of my favorite activities was to take one hundred or so youth out to our church camp on a Friday afternoon after school and give them a weekend of sitting around campfires, singing, learning about the faith, eating great camp food, swimming, and playing but hardly getting any sleep.

It was here that I developed a teaching program called Jesus Alive in an attempt to counterbalance the then popular idea that perhaps God is dead. It was here that I stopped using the word *God* because I too wanted the theistic one, NoOneUpThere, to be "dead." I began using the word *Creation* instead. For me, the word *God* carried a great deal of negative, erroneous luggage. The concept of Creation fit the bill. Creation is not an outside force that makes decisions about all of us on earth—it is an active and continuous force that permeates every facet of the universe. Even though it can seem destructive at times, like during hurricanes or earthquakes, Creation embodies a sense of orderliness. *Higher Power* is also a good phrase for this concept, one often used by people recovering from addiction, but *Creation* is still my operative word for what most others call God.

I wasn't just exploring the idea of God and Creation in my early years in Hawai'i; I also started to develop an image of Jesus as fully human, a down-to-earth man with all the strengths and weaknesses of every other human. This picture was much more attractive to me than some of the strange-looking Jesuses I discuss in chapter 3. I felt like a traitor to the Episcopal church and my ordination vows but knew I was on the right track. I knew that the twentieth-century church needed a historical human Jesus.

Then something happened! A week after I arrived in Hawai'i, I had my first date with Annie, the new kindergarten teacher at the parish's parochial school. She was single and beautiful and had a wonderful smile—still does. The following June we were married at our church, and fifty-six years later, I can assure you that was one of my greatest decisions. But marriage can change one's daily theology as two individuals struggle to become one yet maintain their individuality. It is also a great opportunity to practice agape love.

Off to France

During my trip to Europe after seminary, I fell in love with the French city of Strasbourg, on the northeastern French-German border. Some distant relatives lived there and were very kind to me. I knew that I wanted to return there someday, somehow. In my first summer as a priest, I innocently wrote a letter to the dean of the protestant theological seminary in Strasbourg, asking if the school offered any doctoral degrees in theology. I was discouraged when I received a poorly mimeographed response in French, a language I couldn't read, speak, or understand.

Then came a life-changing letter from the dean of the seminary in Strasbourg. He had never had an Episcopal or Anglican priest in the seminary and wanted to offer me a full scholarship to attend the University of Strasbourg to work on a *doctorate en science religieux* (doctorate in religious science). I could hardly believe it. A year later, off we went—Annie, our nine-month-old daughter, Gretchen; and I—to live in Strasbourg and start a new chapter in our lives.

The title of my thesis to be was "The Influence of the Old Testament on the Birth Narrative in the Gospel of Matthew." Sound familiar? This was very similar to the project that I had started when I had to spend the summer in Berkeley. My tutor, Dr. Trocme, loved the title and the idea. One day early in the process of my working on the thesis, he whispered to me, "Never preach or teach this. You'll be excommunicated." I felt like a real heretic. What would that trial be like? It sounded fun!

While in France, Annie and I decided to grow our family. She became pregnant again, but this time she experienced problems from the beginning. The French doctors had no good answers—only silly solutions from the Middle Ages—so Annie felt that we needed to return to the United States and see an American doctor. By this time, all my coursework at Strasbourg was finished, but we had to leave before I could defend my thesis and earn my doctorate. We moved from Strasbourg, a sophisticated community where life began at 8:00 p.m., to Wailuku, Maui, an agrarian community where life ended at 8:00 p.m. Unfortunately, Annie and I found no solution to the problems with her pregnancy in the United States either. The baby was due in early December, but in mid-January, Annie was still scrubbing floors and washing windows to try to induce labor. Then on January 20, 1965, our second daughter, Heidi, decided it was time to join the real world.

It's Not Fair!

At 4:00 a.m., our little girl emerged looking shriveled, underweight, and overcooked. She was covered with red dots and had a mature cataract on her right eye, another eye issue called a nystagmus, a heart murmur, and more hidden medical challenges that we would discover later, such as severe deafness, epilepsy, and mild cerebral palsy.

Many people believe that NoOneUpThere would purposefully give these afflictions to an innocent baby to punish Annie and me for some misdeed in our past. One person even told us that we were being blessed because we were such wonderful parents and should have the pleasure of raising such a child. When I heard this, I wanted to puke.

Fortunately, I had dealt with a similar issue after the motorcycle accident. I already knew that NoOneUpThere was not orchestrating anything—this is just life, with all its imperfections. We cannot accept life to the fullest until we accept the fact that bad stuff happens no matter what church, temple, or mosque we attend or don't attend. Our responsibility is to learn to deal creatively with these challenges. This book shares tools for doing that.

Heidi is now a high-functioning fifty-two-year-old college graduate, living independently in Seattle, with a good job and a very full life. Please don't feel sorry for her or us. Having Heidi in our lives has been a tremendous growing experience for our family and many who know her. We like to tell people that Heidi's only handicap is that people call her handicapped. She is deaf and legally blind but quick to explain that she is not handicapped but simply has limitations like every other human being.

Another Lemon

A year after Heidi was born, Annie and I decided that I would resign from my parish so that we could move back to Honolulu to provide Heidi with the many services she needed. My rising career in the Episcopal church would be in jeopardy, but Heidi's future was more important than my career.

The new rector of the church where I had started my ministry needed a youth director—the group of 350 that I had left in 1963 had dwindled to 40 young people in just three years. I enjoyed working with teenagers, and although many clergy would consider this transfer a demotion, I gladly accepted the position, providing that I could have carte blanche to create innovative youth programs. Within two years, some 2,500 teens were involved in a large variety of programs, including worship, choirs, bands, theater, sports, and even a coffeehouse.

Everything was going well until our theater program decided to perform an anti–Vietnam War play. Even though the rector had given me carte blanche, he forbade the performance of the play at his church. However, a liberal Congregational church offering sanctuary to soldiers who went AWOL to protest the war asked me if we could perform the play for them in downtown Honolulu.

Our play was well received, but the next morning at 7:00 a.m., the rector found me as I was cleaning the toilets in the youth center (our maintenance man had called in sick), accused me of disobeying his orders, and said, "You're fired! You have thirty days to move you and your family out of the church-provided housing and buy your own car."

I am still working on this one: I was fired from a church, a Christian church, because I was against war. On top of that, the rector had the audacity to treat me and my family as if we were criminals. He made certain that we were totally isolated and told the congregation a lie about why I was leaving.

Many years later, I received a letter from the rector asking for forgiveness. He confessed that he fired me because he was threatened by my success and all the national publicity I had received. A year after he fired me, the youth program at his church had dwindled to under forty—less than the number of members I started with.

Two hours after I was fired, I called the bishop's office and told him what had happened. He replied, "Good! I just hired you to work on my staff."

For the next seven years, I developed a series of ministries with the bishop—who appointed me diocesan youth director—including a shelter for runaway youth, Hale Kipa, a program that is still going strong all over the Islands; a free medical clinic for people without medical insurance or with drug addiction; and a lobbying group for deaf and blind people in Hawai'i. I was also appointed vicar of a dying church in one of the Hawaiian homesteads. At the bishop's request, I began running all the church camps on the Islands and flew to the Marshall Islands once a month to operate a small Episcopal mission on Kwajalein.

In 1974, Annie and I decided we needed to move to Southern California to further Heidi's education. The school we chose was referred to as mainstream because Heidi would have classes with hearing children for part of the day and also classes specifically geared toward students with hearing impairments. Now Heidi would get to live in the real world, which can be rather cruel for people with challenges, rather than the sheltered environment we found at Hawai'i School for the Deaf and Blind.

Things were looking up for my family, but I was looking at a different picture. At forty-three years of age, I had invested my adult life in the Episcopal church for eighteen years. I had been innovative, creative, and hardworking. (But the bishop in Los Angeles, without even looking at my résumé, said he was not interested in interviewing me.)

Fortunately, right after I was fired, I realized that I needed a backup vocation, so I enrolled in the University of Hawai'i to earn my master's degree in social work and urban and regional planning. Smart move!

"What Color Is Your Parachute?"

Let me back up a bit. In Hawai'i, consultants would come from all over the world to "consult," especially when they were having a cold winter where they lived. One of these consultants was Dick Bolles, who was the Episcopal church's national director of college work. Dick loved to come to Hawai'i when it was freezing in New York City, consult with some of the colleges for a few days, and then head to the beach. Dick had written a book, *What Color Is Your*

Parachute? It was about a different way to find a job. I bought his book and worked through the exercises.

I flew to San Francisco for a five-day conference Dick was holding. After three days of classroom work, on the fourth day we practiced our new skills and had to make an appointment to interview the CEO of any company we chose. The next day, we learned that a third of the class had been offered a job by the boss they interviewed. Obviously, the system worked.

The Church—without Pay

Once we had arrived in Santa Ana, California, and unpacked, I started my job search by paying a courtesy call to the bishop of Los Angeles. His secretary said the bishop could see me in a few weeks for ten minutes. I thought, "I have to drive four hours for a ten-minute visit?" When I arrived, I was ushered into the "throne room" for a very superficial chat. The bishop was pleasant, but at the end of ten minutes his secretary walked in and said his next appointment was waiting. With that, the bishop stood, put his hand out to shake mine, and said, "Good luck in finding a secular job, and don't let me catch you hanging around any sacristies," insinuating that he didn't want me to look for jobs in any of his churches behind his back. I couldn't believe what he had said to me. I remember walking down a major street in Los Angeles with tears streaming down my face, wondering what I had done to deserve that treatment from a bishop.

I continued my search, poring over the help-wanted ads in the newspaper every day. I had never applied for a job before—the Marines and the church simply assigned me. Then one day, I saw a fascinating job advertised by a nearby city, La Mirada, that wanted someone to plan and develop a human services delivery system. With a master's degree in social work and regional and urban planning, this was right up my alley. Although I was brand new to

California, had never worked in government, and had no local references, I decided to apply. My faith constantly gives me the courage to creatively face all the challenges thrown my way.

This job position demanded a Dick Bolles approach, so I called and tried to make an appointment with the city manager to talk about working in city government. His secretary immediately replied that he was extremely busy looking over two hundred applications for a new job position. That meant it was time for plan B.

A few days later, dressed in my coat and tie, I drove to the La Mirada city hall, went into the lobby, and waited for the perfect opportunity. I watched as an official-looking man entered the lobby, and the receptionist greeted him: "Hello, Mr. Klug." There he was—the city manager. I had to pounce, so I marched over to Mr. Klug, introduced myself, and said that I had just moved from Hawai'i to Santa Ana. I shared that I wanted to get into human services in city government and wondered if he could spare half an hour to offer some suggestions.

Hawai'i was the magic word—he and his wife loved the Islands. He said, "Yes, I have some time. Please come into my office and let's chat." It worked! Once in his office, I kept firing questions at him so he would talk about himself and Hawai'i—for an hour and a half. At the end, he said, "You ought to apply for this job."

Thank you, Dick Bolles. *Parachute* worked.

After three weeks, I called the city and was told that now there were over four hundred applications and the final decision would be delayed by two or three weeks. That meant I had to take another job I had been offered, but six weeks into the new job, La Mirada city hall called to schedule an interview. I was offered the job during my interview and resigned from the job I had taken in the meantime.

My new job was great—it paid well and challenged my creativity. But after three years, I was becoming bored with my work. I had taken the development of human services as far as it could go for a small city. I had to face the reality that I'm great at creating and developing ideas, but maintaining them isn't challenging enough.

For three months, I worked with a headhunter who suggested that I start my own company. At first, I worried that my educational background gave me no foundation for starting or maintaining a business, but I finally realized that I'm at my best when my creativity is challenged and I'm not held back by rules, procedures, caution, and procrastination.

I started thinking about what kind of business I could start. It had to be different, it had to use all my gifts and skills, and it had to be challenging.

People Helpers, Inc.

At that time, the state of California, as well as the country, was going through financial hard times, and La Mirada was a city that kept its staff small and contracted almost all services—police, fire, and maintenance work—to outside agencies. I suggested to the city manager that I could save the city about a third of what it paid me if it contracted me to run its human services. He jumped on the idea immediately, and People Helpers, Inc., became a legal California corporation. I was the president and Annie the vice president.

I secured additional contracts in human services, recreational services, and the new wave of childcare services provided before and after school. When I didn't know enough or have enough experience, I asked young, creative, like-minded people to join the company. People Helpers developed into a million-dollar corporation with contracts spread throughout the Los Angeles basin, employing some 125 people.

Starting a business was risky, but I am ever so grateful that my faith gives me the fearlessness to try new ventures and then use my creativity to make them happen.

Not Again!

Life was good. I had a flourishing business and a nice home, Heidi was doing well, and our other two daughters were settled in, so on the weekends I had time to do some fill-in church work. Then, in 1982, our parish had to do some quick reorganization. The rector had been caught in sexually inappropriate behavior and he had to leave in a hurry. The church now needed a part-time fill-in priest to run the Sunday school, develop adult programs, assist with conducting worship, and preach. I was offered and accepted the position.

My preaching was provocative but not too provocative. I had my detractors, but for the most part, people appreciated my energy. (Creativity always attracts naysayers.)

After eighteen months, the search committee found a new rector, whose credentials were outstanding. He had a doctorate, had written a book, was a good preacher and an excellent organizer, and loved doing pastoral work—or at least that's what his résumé said.

Within a few months, however, people started complaining to me about him. At first, I just listened. But people kept saying the same thing, so I decided to go to him, and in the privacy of his office, behind a closed door, I shared, very respectfully, what I was hearing. He didn't like it and treated me as the enemy for the next year.

Six days before Christmas in 1988, he called me into his office and fired me. Not good timing! I decided to go on vacation over the holidays, and when I returned I learned that a movement had started to get rid of the rector. He was gone in six months.

However, the bishop of Los Angeles felt sorry for this man, now jobless, and invited him to work at the diocesan headquarters. Being at the hub of operations, my old "boss" was able to spread unbelievable lies about what had happened. He told people that I had masterminded the whole sequence of events and was secretly funding it. Quite a few clergy bought into his story. To make matters worse, four Episcopal churches, including the one we were attending, told me that I was no longer welcome. One clergyperson ordered me out of his office using language that would make a Marine Corps drill sergeant blush.

We Transfer Our Membership to St. Mattress

Annie and I decided to join another church. It's a very popular one and has many more members than the institutional church. Its name: St. Mattress or St. Sack's. At such a church, one stays in bed on Sunday mornings, reads the newspaper (scripture), drinks coffee, eats freshly baked muffins (communion), watches *Religion & Ethics News Weekly* on television (sermon), and then goes for a long walk (prayers). It was a great experience, but we missed being part of a faith-based community.

During this time, I became involved in the Orange County Interfaith Coalition, where I could rub elbows with Native Americans, Mormons, Muslims, Friends, Baha'is, and people of other Christian denominations, including some fundamentalists. We all shared a love and concern for our fellow human beings, no matter what our faith base was. This was an eye-opening great experience.

Annie and I started looking for a church that was open and affirming to all. Then we found our place at a nearby Episcopal church. Over a period of three years, the rector invited me to teach an adult class, assist with the Eucharist, preach, be the chaplain for the children's Sunday school, and finally, take over the pastoral responsibilities. I accepted each time but became concerned when I realized that the rector would come to the office about nine o'clock and immediately go downstairs to a tiny office and lock himself in there until about two o'clock. This seemed to be his daily routine, and for this he received a rather large salary.

One Monday morning, the rector was late for a staff meeting. Finally, he came storming in, saying rather loudly that he hated this job, with some expletives thrown in. Then I caught wind of another incident in which the rector had physically pushed a vestry person in the midst of a heated discussion. This situation was getting out of hand. I felt it was my duty to speak to one of the diocesan bishops about the rector, but the bishop told me that it was none of my business.

I'd had enough! I tendered my resignation and went back to St. Mattress.

Annie and I had become "church damaged." For fifty years, the institutional church had tried to beat the life out of me. I was still a committed Follower of Jesus, but I found it increasingly difficult to be one within the institutional church.

Total Masochists: We Go Back to Church

I turned my energy toward meditating daily, reading challenging books on theology, and completing my second book, *What's Love Got to Do with It? "Everything!" Says Jesus.* The book showed great growth in my faith since my first book, but it didn't do well in the marketplace. I couldn't find anyone who would review it, which was the key to moving on to the next step in the publishing world.

In the process of marketing my book, I called a pastor whom I had known since the early 1990s when I was cochair of the Orange County Interfaith Coalition. He asked me where we were going to church, and I gave him my standard reply: "St. Mattress." He understood.

He suggested that I try his previous church, Irvine United Congregational Church (IUCC). It was probably not as progressive as I was, but it certainly had many features that I might find attractive: the pastor was an excellent preacher, the congregation was designated "Open and Affirming," there were no creeds, communion was open to all, the church had a great choir and music, people were not afraid to ask hard questions and expect good answers, and it wasn't that far away from where we lived.

As comfortable as St. Mattress was, we decided to try IUCC. Our first Sunday was a bit uncomfortable, with an unfamiliar liturgy, different hymns, and nothing but strangers, but the preacher was excellent. (He is gay with a longtime partner.) This is the church of the future—diverse and open to all "no matter where you are in your life's journey." We joined IUCC, and nine years later we are still members.

I know that my theology is still a bit avant-garde, even to a progressive church like IUCC, so I try to be gentle in sharing it. I now feel most comfortable with IUCC's informal liturgy and have accepted some leadership roles there. Although I have come a long way since my early days in the Episcopal church, I still have lots of growing to do.

Many years ago, Bishop Spong—one of my favorite humanists, teachers, and role models—included this piece by David Keighley, an English Anglican priest, in his weekly newsletter:

Leaving Home

I'm off!

I must leave the political and ethical compromises that have corrupted the faith of my Jesus.

I must leave the stifling theology, the patriarchal structures.

I must leave the enduring prejudices based on our God-given humanity, the colour of my skin, my gender or how my sexual orientation is practiced.

I must leave the mentality that encourages anyone to think that our doctrines are unchangeable.

I must leave the belief of those who insist that our sacred texts are without error.

I must leave the God of miracle and magic.

I must leave the promises of certainty, the illusion of possessing the true faith.

I must leave behind the claims of being the recipient of an unchallengeable revelation.

I must leave the neurotic religious desire to know that I am right, and to play at being God.

I must leave the claim that every pathway to God is second-rate, that fellow Hindu searchers in India, Buddhists in China and Tibet, Muslims in the Middle East and the Jews of Israel are inadequate.

I must leave the pathway that tells me that all other directions will get me lost.

I must leave the certain claim that my Jesus is the only way to God for everyone.

I must leave the Church, my home.

I must leave behind my familiar creeds and faith-symbols.

I can no longer stay in an unlivable space.

I must move to a place where I can once again sing the Lord's song.

I must move to where my faith-tradition can be revived and live on.

I must move to a place where children don't tell me what I belief is unbelievable but tell me they can believe what I believe.

I must move to a place where they are not playing at moving the deck chairs on the decks of an ecclesiastical Titanic.

I can never leave the God experience.

I can never walk away from the doorway into the divine that I believe I have found in the one I call the Christ and acknowledge as "my Lord."

I must move to dangerous and religiously threatening places.

I must move to where there is no theism, but still God.
I'm off! But to where, God only knows.[1]

I meditate on this piece every Friday morning because it helps motivate me in my continuing faith journey. Our earth and the universe have made great strides since I came into it in 1932. Unfortunately, the church has not. I want it to because it has great tools as found in Jesus's message and agape love.

> *Don't be afraid to think differently from the people around you. Be afraid of what will be lost because you were afraid to think, rethink and think again of ways to make what is now necessary, real.*
> —Sister Joan Chittister, *The Monastic Way*

CHAPTER 2

Food for Thot

It's frustrating when you know all the answers
but nobody asks you the questions.
—Unknown

In chapter 1, I shared my Christian upbringing and the progression of my theological thinking, primarily for the past sixty years. I've come a long way from where I started. Some, perhaps many, would say that I have come too far. Others would accuse me of no longer being a Christian but closer to a Unitarian or even an agnostic. A few might tell me I am a heretic or even go as far as to say that I am an atheist.

Whatever! (My favorite prayer!) I know that I am a Follower of Jesus and a practicing one, no matter what anyone says.

Although I was raised Christian, in no way do I believe that Christianity is the only true faith. Every religion has part of the answer—some more than others, but that's subjective.

Even though this entire book is food for thought, I have chosen twenty subjects to discuss in this chapter, hoping that my ideas might trigger some reactions from you—either negative or positive. In no way do I believe I have all, or even any, of the answers, but I suspect you will have your own ideas. For me, that is what keeps the world interesting and how we learn.

1. Creation, Yes! God, No!

A ten-year-old girl was working intently on a drawing in her art class when her teacher came up behind her and asked, "Mary, what are you working so hard on?"

Mary responded, "I'm drawing a picture of God." The teacher was a bit taken aback and responded, "But Mary, no one knows what God looks like." Without hesitating, Mary replied, "You will in a moment."

For the first twenty-three years of my life, I also thought I knew what God looked like. He was a he—sort of like a superman who was feared by all and who could decide where we would spend eternity.

Then the fire engine hit me and killed Brad. I knew that if NoOneUpThere was causing hideous things like this, I wanted no part of this religion. Shortly after finishing seminary, I started substituting the word *Creation* for *God*. It felt good. Creation is not anthropomorphic, has no gender, and is everywhere in the universe—it's you and me. It doesn't have a son and is uninhibited by time or space. It simply is there. Creation does not run our lives on a daily basis, is not the Master Puppeteer, Celestial Traffic Director, or Heavenly Santa Claus.

In 1990, the Hubble Space Telescope was launched. It has yet to find heaven or hell, but it gives us small hints as to the vastness of the universe, beyond human comprehension.

I think God is an invention of humanity, but I do believe in the force of Creation. Paul Tillich, a famous twentieth-century theologian, calls that force "the ground of all being."[1] Groups like Alcoholics Anonymous call it Supreme Being.

Let's be honest: no one really knows.

2. What's a Christian A-Theist?

I'm a Christian a-theist—an oxymoron if I ever heard one. I put a hyphen between the *a* and the *theist* for two reasons: (1) I want to grab your attention, and (2) *a* means "against"—I am opposed to theism, which denotes "a personal God who creates, preserves and governs the world."[2] It's a total fabrication that the institutional church continues to market.

I find being an a-theist very liberating. It clears away almost all the antiquated, irrelevant dogma and doctrine and allows us to see Jesus as the prophet or sage he really was and to practice what he preached.

3. Is It a Ghost or a Spirit?

Growing up, I equated the Holy Ghost with Halloween. When I arrived at seminary, the church was going through liturgical upgrades and *Ghost* became *Spirit*, a much better word. But what or who is it?

Here's my take: it's the Spirit of Agape. I think every human being, even those deemed "horrible" by society, possess that Spirit. But too many times, the church and our society never teach that. They're too busy reminding everyone how bad they are. The Spirit of Agape reminds people how good they can be.

4. Three in One

I remember as a child using a shoe polish whose claim to fame was that it did three different jobs: clean, shine, and protect. Not surprisingly, it was called 3 in 1.

Christians also have a three-in-one product. It's called the Trinity: one God but three different natures: Father, Son, and Holy Ghost. After the church fathers settled on this doctrine, if anyone had problems accepting the Trinity, the person was either excommunicated or executed—in the name of Jesus.

As a child and young man, I never questioned the Trinity. I wasn't allowed to, nor did I have enough information to do so. In seminary, we were forced to buy into it, and after I was ordained, I kept on defending it, as if I understood it. I dreaded having to preach about nonsense on Trinity Sunday. Fortunately, the Trinity is a casualty of the death of theism. May it rest in peace!

Here's my twenty-first-century take on this concept: God is Creation; Jesus is one of the more Creative people in history, and the Holy Spirit is the Creation within each and every one of us. Jesus gives us the tool of agape, which we can use to exercise the Creativity within us.

5. My Least Favorite Word: *Sin*

Too many Christians love the word *sin* and want to remind us that we are all sinners and in great need of being saved. When I was a young Episcopalian, *The Book of Common Prayer* would make me say in the Holy Communion liturgy that "we are unworthy to gather up the crumbs under thy Table."[3] Am I really that bad?

In seminary, we talked a great deal about sin. It's too bad we didn't talk as much about goodness. So when I was working with teenagers, I did *not* want to remind them one more time that they were inadequate. Their parents, siblings, teachers, relatives, neighbors, and peers did enough of that. I wanted to tell them how good they were and that they were filled with the spirit of agape.

So, I started using the word *separation*, something we all go through, either knowingly or unknowingly, with ourselves and others. I would like to see the word *sin* excommunicated, and in its place we could talk about people's goodness and how we can heal separation.

6. To Hell with Hell

When I was growing up, hell was a very hot place DownThere, with a devil in charge. All the people I know were certain they were going there. I don't think I have ever met anyone who said that he or she was a "slam dunk" for heaven.

But by the time I was ordained and had started teaching, I began thinking of hell as more of a way of living than a place. Ask drug addicts, people in prison, or prostitutes if they feel they live in heaven or hell.

7. Judgment

For many, Christianity seems to be all about judgment, both during our lives and after we die. Too many churches love to judge. They know their god hates anyone in the LGBTQ community, divorcees, women who have had an abortion, Muslims, Jews (they killed Jesus), and so on.

Many Christians believe that on Judgment Day, "Chief Justice" Peter will decide to send us either Up or Down. Fortunately, all that malarkey went the way of theism.

On the other hand, judgment is important for our survival. For example, to be a good defensive automobile driver, I must be judgmental about the drivers all around me: Is that driver texting? Is this one an older person who seems unsure? How about that car racing down the freeway at one hundred miles an hour? Is it a police pursuit or someone on drugs? Or could it be a person rushing someone to the hospital? Whatever the situation, I have to make a judgment and do something.

My survival depends on being judgmental, but I need some guidelines. I must ask myself, What are my prejudices and biases? Am I able to rise above my biases and practice agape? Will I be able to love those whom other members of society might call the lepers or outcasts? Can I accept the fact that others will make some rather heavy judgments about me? Judgment is here to stay, but Followers need to be very careful about how and when we use it.

8. Atonement versus At-One-Ment

The words *atonement* and *at-one-ment* might look similar, but they are vastly different.

For Christians, atonement is the idea that Jesus died for—atoned for—our sins by giving his life on the Cross.

I find this concept problematic for several reasons: it is human sacrifice, it is barbaric, and it is total fantasy to suggest that a father would plan to have his son murdered for "my sins." Then for the institutional church to even suggest that I have to buy into this sort of horrendous thinking is an insult to my intelligence and sense of morality.

My first bishop introduced me to the idea of at-one-ment, pronounced "at one ment." It's my ticket to a fuller, richer life. The basic concept is that as a Follower, my duty and responsibility is to learn to be "at one" with myself, my neighbor, and Creation.

9. The Bible

The Bible is often referred to as the bestseller that hardly anyone reads.

I read it every day and think I am qualified to say that it has more violence than anyone needs. For the most part, it's not very interesting. Some of its advice is badly outdated, and some of it is just plain boring.

I read the entire Bible for the first time in my life, in seminary, at the age of twenty-five, under the supervision of my professors. They explained how it was written, when it was written, who wrote it, why it was written, the languages in which it was written, and how it was put together. It was all very fascinating, but I still find much of the Bible difficult to read and understand, so I have all sorts of resource materials to assist me.

It was in the fourth century of the Common Era that a group of church folks picked and chose the books they felt told the story the way they wanted it told. We have no idea how many books they had to choose from, but as of 2014, we knew of 127 different manuscripts that could have been chosen. New ones seem to pop up periodically.

Some books of the Bible don't make any sense to me. The book of Revelation tops the list, and I have sworn off it for the rest of my life. I also rarely preach from the Old Testament—I worry that I would put a Christian spin on it because of my limited knowledge about Judaism. I call myself a New Testament Christian.

Even though I prefer some books of the Bible over others and read the Bible daily, I keep finding information I missed during the last fifty-five-plus years. Taking the Bible literally is a mistake. It is not a book about history, but it is a book about great truth often wrapped in an attention-grabbing story.

10. Saul/Paul: Asset or Liability?

As a child, I loved to study maps of St. Paul's traveling adventures. I heard about his life through stories from the book of Acts, and he sounded like an interesting person.

In seminary, I went so far as to read some of his letters in Greek—the Greek of antiquity, when writers did not use punctuation, capitalization, or paragraphs. That's quite a challenge.

Paul, whose Jewish name was Saul, was a great, dedicated missionary who endured hardship to spread the Good News to the Jews in the Diaspora, but over the years, I began to dislike him. I started learning about Paul's early emphasis on a Second Coming, his condescending attitude toward women, his advice concerning marriage, and his ideas about Jesus dying for our sins.

Two thousand years later, people are still spouting his message that Jesus died for our sins. Consequently, many Christians spend much of their life groveling and not nearly enough time doing things for "the least of these" (Matt. 25:45)—Jesus's true message. Paul's message about Jesus dying on a cross for our sins seemed to arouse a great deal of interest around the world and made Christianity a powerful, dominating religion.

Had Paul simply marketed Jesus as the epitome of agape, I am not so sure that this message would have flown. I strongly suspect that the early Jesus movement would have simply faded away within the first generation had it not included atonement theology. That seemed to be a big selling point for the early church, and I guess it still is in some sectors. In the long run, I'm forced to see Paul as neither an asset nor a liability. He's a dichotomy.

11. Devils, Angels, Seraphim, Cherubim, Satan, and All Other Imaginary Beings

We've all heard the expressions "The devil made me do it!" and "I have a guardian angel." I can never figure out why people need these fictitious beings. Religion has used such figments of the imagination to make unbelievable, inexplicable things happen. The Bible and Christian art and folklore are full of characters that suddenly appear and give messages straight from NoOneUpThere. But these imaginary beings distract us from what we really need to be doing, "loving the least of these" (Matt. 25:45).

12. Mary

Growing up, I respected the fact that Mary was the mother of Jesus. I probably even bought into the idea that she was a virgin and that God impregnated her. (I never was very good at biology.) I loved Christmas, the religious services, the birth of Jesus, the decorations, and of course, the gifts.

In seminary, I was able to take a better look at Mary in the context of the New Testament and the times. In Mary's time, women had children at a very young age, primarily for economic reasons because Mom and Dad needed all the help they could find to do daily chores and support their jobs.

The stories of Jesus's birth are confusing, especially if taken literally. Only Matthew and Luke tell an infancy narrative, and their stories are as different as night and day, although both suggest that heavenly help was involved. On the other hand, the Gospel of John states in two separate instances that Joseph was the father of Jesus.

One possibility is that Mary somehow became pregnant out of wedlock and, no longer a virgin, was unwanted property, so Joseph bought her for a bargain. Or perhaps Matthew's and Luke's stories are figments of their imagination invented so that Jesus would not be considered a bastard. Yet another option is that the birth narratives are metaphors. Of these possibilities, the last choice makes the most sense—but it doesn't make an iota of difference to me. Jesus is my Christ because of his message, not because of who got Mary pregnant.

I am always disappointed in Mary's reactions. The scriptures paint her as passive when Jesus was being stoned. Most mothers I know would not have quietly allowed others to hurt their children. According to the synoptic gospels (Mathew, Mark, and Luke), Mary wasn't at the crucifixion or the resurrection, despite the artists who included her in the last events of the Jesus story, like Michelangelo did in his statue *Pietà*. The Gospel of John, written eighty years after Jesus's murder, places Mary at the foot of the cross, but I am more inclined to believe the synoptic writers than the author of John.

I dislike Mariology not because of who Mary was but because of what the institutional church has made her out to be. In many Christian churches around the world, Mary has become more important than her son. In my eyes and the synoptic gospels, Mary is hardly important in the big picture, and she distracts us from carrying out what Jesus wants us to do with our lives. My theory about why people idolize Mary is that she is much easier to follow than Jesus—she expects nothing of her groupies and allows them to remain in the "comfortable pew." On the other hand, Jesus has great expectations and demands for his Followers, and his "pew" can be most uncomfortable.

If women need an exemplary female role model, take a hard look at Mary of Magdala, or Mary Magdalene, a dynamo who was always there for Jesus.

13. Midrash

In seminary, I understood the concept of looking for the meaning in a story, but I had never heard the Hebrew word *midrash*, which comes from a word meaning "to interpret." I like the concept of investigating the many possible ideas that a story could be communicating. As far as I'm concerned, it's the only way one can make sense of most of the stories in the Bible.

For example, the story of Jesus told in Mark (6:45–52) and Matthew (14:22–33) is not about Jesus doing hocus-pocus and defying nature, as Jesus is reputed to have walked on water, in a storm, to meet his terrified disciples. That is a fairy tale. The story has a much deeper meaning. My interpretation is that the storm relates to the storms in life, and the disciples represent you and me—they became terrified just as we do when a storm hits. Jesus comes to Peter, who has tried and failed to walk on the water himself, and says, "O man of little faith, why did you doubt?" (Matt. 14:31) I don't think doubt was the issue, but belief was his problem. Peter's belief wasn't strong enough. This story always leads me to ask myself whether my faith is deep enough and strong enough.

Using midrash, other people might find different meanings to this story, depending on their life experiences and interpretations.

14. Prayer

Because of my different theology, people have asked me if I pray. For the first twenty-five years of my life, I prayed only when I was in trouble and would ask NoOneUpThere to rescue me. I must have always had a poor connection because I never received an answer. But now I pray every morning because I feel a tremendous need to prepare for each day. I call this my quiet time: I get out of bed around five—the house stays quiet until about seven, when Annie gets up—I make coffee, sit at my desk, and start my quiet time with a series of reminders in the shape of a cross.

I start at the top of the cross (or plus sign, see number 18) and focus on thoughts of praise, such as "I love life" or "Creation is wonderful!" Then I move to the left side of the cross, where I list everything I am thankful for. It's a very long list, reminding me how privileged I am to have good health, a wonderful wife of fifty-five-plus years, a supportive family, a creative mind, and many rich opportunities to enhance my life.

I then move to the center of the cross, where I remember all the members of our family one by one. Regardless of my political persuasion, I remember the president, the governor of California, and the mayor of our city. Having worked in government, I am well aware of all the effort most politicians put in, whether I agree with them or not. I also have a special list of those who are sick, terminal, housebound, or incarcerated or have other challenging issues. This list changes all the time. It not only helps me remember people but serves as a reminder that as a Follower I need to make contact with those people on a periodic basis.

Then I go to the right side of the cross, where I am forced to face my own shortcomings. I can clearly see how immature, insensitive, and unloving my behavior can be at times, and I need to correct it. At the bottom, I have my list of traits I need to develop. On top of the list is always *Patience*, for which I have been praying to improve for over fifty years. I think I am finally doing much better. Or maybe it's just that I'm tired. Next on my list is *Humility,* of which I can always use more.

Then I read and study a selection from the Bible, books like Bishop Spong's *Biblical Literalism: A Gentile Heresy,* and provocative articles from religious magazines such as *Sojourners* and *The 4th R.* This takes me about an hour and seems to center me for the day.

15. The Lord's Prayer

In the Episcopal church's *Book of Common Prayer,* we address NoOneUpThere as "Our Father, who art in heaven,"[4] as if there is a heaven and someone lives in it. Next, we tell that imaginary being in that imaginary place what he has to do. I am always a bit confused whether we are ordering or begging NoOneUpThere to "Give us . . . our daily bread . . . forgive us . . . lead us not into temptation, but deliver us from evil."[5] In reality, you and I need to provide our own daily bread, forgive ourselves and others, and have the basic tools to stay out of temptation's way.

The version of the so-called Lord's Prayer we use today isn't anything like the Lord's Prayer in Matthew and Luke. Luke's version (11:2–4) goes "Father, hallowed be thy name. Thy kingdom come. Give us each day our daily bread; and forgive us our sins, for we ourselves forgive everyone who is indebted to us; and lead us not into temptation." This version is much shorter than today's, but it still suggests that NoOneUpThere is going to do everything we ask.

I found this modern version of the so-called Lord's Prayer. I call it The Jesus Prayer, not because Jesus actually said these words but because the prayer represents what he taught:

> O presence and power within us,
> being and light of all.
> How we are filled,

how we o'erflow
with infinite love and gladness!
We shall this day sow grace and peace,
and show mercy to all,
and gentle loving-kindness. And we shall not be so
self-serving,
but a constant source of giving.
For ours is the essence,
and the wholeness, and the fullness forever. Amen.[6]

I'm not telling NoOneUpThere what to do. I'm telling myself on a daily basis what I have to do to help bring the Kingdom of God, the Kingdom of Love, into existence.

16. The Creeds

My definition of a creed is "a formal statement of religious belief." I sort of understand why the church feels it needs to have creeds but would ask, Why does the church force members to make outrageous statements that have no validity? As a child and young man, with my eyes closed, I used to love to recite the creeds by memory, but in the 1990s, I realized I hardly believed a word of the creeds.

Let's take a look at the Nicene Creed. The congregation states, "We believe in God, the Father almighty, creator of heaven and earth." I don't believe it. They go on to state that God had an "only Son, our Lord." I would never call Jesus my Lord. In my vocabulary, the term *lord* is feudalistic, implying a man with lots of power who takes advantage of the poor for his own gain and is always looking for a war. Then creed sayers declare: "He was conceived by the power of the Holy Spirit and born of the Virgin Mary." Today, this would be considered child abuse and biologically impossible.

This is the only statement that has some truth: "He suffered under Pontius Pilate, was crucified dead and was buried." People have been saying this for over seventeen hundred years, but some churchgoers still believe that the Jews killed Jesus. Others espouse that Jesus swooned on the cross and didn't really die. He disappeared and hid for the rest of his life. Others believe Pilate, being corrupt, was paid off and another body was substituted. Conspiracy theories run wild.

Then the creed continues: "He descended to the dead. On the third day he rose again. He ascended into heaven, and is seated on the right hand of the Father. He will come again to judge the living and the dead." That's nothing but silly.

Finally, the congregation says, "We believe in the Holy Spirit, the holy Catholic [meaning universal] Church, the communion of saints, the forgiveness of sins, the resurrection of the body, and the life everlasting." I do believe in forgiveness, but for me, this life is all there is. Many think there's more, want more, don't want life to end, believe whatever the church tells them, or don't think about the subject. I have thought about it for over sixty years and agree with Genesis 3:19: "By the sweat of your face you shall eat bread until you return to the ground, for out of it you were taken; you are dust, and to dust you shall return."

17. Christmas: Bah, Humbug!

One of my favorite secular holidays is Christmas. My least favorite Christian festival is Christmas.

In 336 CE, Emperor Constantine declared December 25 as the day Jesus was born. It is said that he chose this date to oppose a drunken Roman holiday. (I wonder if that worked.) But no one has any idea when Jesus was born because in Jesus's time, birthdays weren't celebrated. Some guesstimaters suggest that Jesus was born in the spring. The Eastern church doesn't even recognize December 25 as a holiday. Instead, members celebrate Epiphany, January 6, as the day the wise men recognized Jesus as "the newborn king." Paul, Mark, and John don't even mention a birth story.

I have some theological issues with celebrating the so-called birth of Jesus on December 25. Not only do we not know when Jesus was born, but the powerful message of Jesus is not about a cute, cuddly little baby lying in a manger. It's about agape—loving the hurting world 24/7 every day of our lives. In addition, we live in a multiracial, multicultural, multireligious world. To demand that the rest of the world stop because Christians are celebrating a non-event is rather insensitive. Our country doesn't close down for any other religion's high feast days. So instead of celebrating Christmas, why not celebrate winter solstice during the same period—a holiday for everyone, religious or not?

18. Why a Cross?

For years, I had no problem with a cross being a symbol of Christianity. I used to wear one around my neck when vested and had an extensive collection of crosses from all over the world.

Then I started thinking about the symbolism of a cross, a weapon of torture, pain, and suffering. With the elimination of theism, one can see very clearly that Jesus and his Followers were about agape and healing. I see the image of a dove, a symbol of peace, being much closer to what I believe. (See my book cover.)

When I see people wearing a cross, I always wonder what it means to them. When we lived in Hawai'i, the bishop had a secretary who went to church every day; acted very holy; had a somber, stern demeanor; and wore a cross necklace and earrings—but behind that cloak was a woman meaner than a junkyard dog. Out with crosses, in with doves.

19. Fundamentalism

I first became aware of fundamentalists and fundamentalism in the 1960s when I hired a group of them, all recovering from drug abuse, to be my kitchen and maintenance staff at the Episcopal

Church Camp at Mokuleia on the island of Oahu in Hawai'i. They seemed to have a difficult time doing what they were supposed to do, and after one of them, the camp cook, pushed his wife off a second-floor balcony because she disobeyed him, I had to let all of them go.

Today, fundamentalists are a powerful force in the world both in religion and in politics. We live in Orange County, California, where we have quite a few megachurches that are packed with fundamentalists, almost all of whom are Republicans. The fundamentalist Christians in our country seem to avoid the word *fundamental*. I wonder why? Maybe because they know it symbolizes narrowness, bigotry, hatred, control, and sexism. They have now usurped the words *evangelistic*, *evangelical*, and *evangelism*, I guess in an attempt to cover who they are and what they believe.

I know fundamentalists. They interpret the Bible literally, "talk" with God and Jesus, all believe the same thing, use the same sort of religious lingo, and will get rid of anyone who doesn't fall within their rather tight definition of who can be a Christian. I have had my share of lectures from fundamentalists, but sadly, I have never had a meaningful discussion with even one.

20. Am I a Christian?

Most of my life I have been told I am not a Christian. When I was growing up, the Roman Catholics told me that I could not go to their church because only Roman Catholics were allowed to receive sacraments, and they could definitely not come to mine. I think it is a mortal sin for them to attend our church for any reason other than a funeral or wedding. If I went to their church, I would have to just sit there and not participate—except at Father Tom's church in Carol Stream. The Roman Catholic Church continues to cover up the molestation of children and at the same time claims to be the one true Christian church. Gimme a break!

The fundamentalists tell me I'm not a Christian because I haven't been born again, I don't believe God wrote the Bible, I don't believe NoOneUpThere is micromanaging the universe, I don't take the Bible literally, and I don't subscribe to intelligent design.

Some Christians say that because I believe every human being (even sex offenders, mass murderers, and Hitler) is invited to be a member of the Kingdom of God, I am not a Christian. They see me as a heretic because I think outside the box—but Jesus taught me to do that. As Sister Joan Chittister wrote, "Searching for new answers is not infidelity or heresy or treason. It is the gateway to the fulfillment of what it means to be human."[7]

My definition of *Christian* starts with the breakdown of the word itself: it starts with *Christ* and ends with *ian*, signifying one who adheres to Christ. In the Marine Corps, at the age of twenty-two, I chose my Christ. He was a lifelong dedicated Jew, totally human, whose life was cut short some two thousand years ago. This man was charismatic with a deep understanding of humanity. I see him as a quiet, radical revolutionary who changed the world without firing a shot. Call me whatever you want, but I'm going to continue to call Jesus my Christ.

In one of his provocative books, Bishop Spong explains "why Christianity must change or die." This is not only the title of his book but reality staring us in the face. Christianity has to change! Twenty-first century thinkers don't buy into a theistic god and all the dogma and doctrine built on that idea—that belief system is left over from the fourth century, and it doesn't fly anymore. For Christianity to remain relevant—and more importantly, for Jesus's message to continue reaching people and giving them the tools to improve our lives, our communities, and our world through agape—we need to have the courage to question the messages the church gives us. We need to learn to think for ourselves, just like

Jesus did, and keep challenging the church to join the twenty-first century.

> *"Because we've always done it that way" is the death knell of life. Avoid it like the plague.*
> —Sister Joan Chittister, *The Art of Life*

PART II

MEETING THE REAL JESUS

CHAPTER 3

Which Jesus?

Jesus was born because Mary had an immaculate contraption.
The people who followed the Lord were called the 12 decibels.
It was a miracle when Jesus rose from the dead and
managed to get the tombstone off the entrance.
—Answers from a Roman Catholic elementary school test

People are surprised when I suggest that there are many versions of Jesus: the mystical Jesus, the mythical Jesus, the magical Jesus, the bizarre Jesus, the combo Jesus, and the historical Jesus. Allow me to elaborate.

The Mystical Jesus

For the Followers of the mystical Jesus, practically everything he does or says is a mystery. They say, "We don't understand it. We don't need to. Miracles don't need any explanation. They are part of the mystery of God."

As the story goes, Jesus is God incarnate who came down from UpThere. He looks and acts like a man, but he is really God. His conception and birth stories don't need an explanation—all we have to do is believe that NoOneUpThere came down and penetrated a teenage girl, who became pregnant and gave birth to the Son of God. Although this is a story about the rape of a minor, God can do that!

I remember a portrait of the mystical Jesus in my father's church in Philadelphia. The painting was about ten feet high and eight feet wide. In this painting, Jesus had smooth, white skin, rosy cheeks, and ruby-red lips. His long brown hair, almost shoulder length, was perfectly coiffed, a pageboy with streaks of blond blended in. He was wearing a tunic underneath his rather expensive-looking top layer, which was a burgundy silk fabric. None of his clothing was wrinkled. His manicured white hands, with long fingernails, were stretched out in a welcoming gesture. His white feet were bare, pedicured, and raised about six inches off the ground.

Never in my wildest dreams would I envision that a Middle Eastern Jewish man from peasant stock who spent too much time in the hot sun looked like this, as if he had migrated from Sweden. I am not sure why people would ever picture Jesus looking like a well-heeled Scandinavian instead of a person from the Middle East unless they needed their God and his entourage to appear to be privileged white folks. I guess the mystical Jesus's white appearance must just be another mystery for which his Followers don't need an explanation.

The Mythical Jesus

Jesus died sometime between 30 and 33 CE. The first written information we have about Jesus is from Paul's letters, dated from the early 40s until Paul died in about 63 CE. This is at least ten years after the death of Jesus, and we all know what time does with facts. It's obvious that Paul knew about a person named Jesus but knew nothing of his personal life. I'm sure the myth building had started by that time, but Paul decided early on to characterize Jesus as the leader of the Second Coming. When that story didn't happen, Jesus then became the Son of God and the sacrificial Lamb who died for our sins. This myth still permeates Christianity.

Mark came on the scene about 70 CE, followed by Matthew, then Luke, and finally John over a span of thirty to forty years. Each of the authors has his own stories as well as some that are similar to others' stories. In a period of about seventy years, the historical

Jesus became the mythical Jesus, promoted from fellow human to God. I have a few ideas about how this happened. As stories are passed on in an oral tradition, the teller inadvertently omits or adds some words. Some of this is unintentional, just little mistakes, but some of it is very intentional to perhaps help support the bias of the author. Entire stories have been added to Jesus's life, such as the two birth narratives or the four or five resurrection tales. Another possibility is that the stories were invented or reworked so that the life of Jesus corresponded to many of the prophesies or stories in the Old Testament.

Adapting Jesus's story was easy because most listeners were illiterate and wouldn't know the difference. There were no fact checkers, and when an authority figure said something was true, one didn't argue. On the other hand, Jewish Followers understood how to use midrash (interpretation) to find the gem of wisdom inside a story that probably was the truth.

Let me share an example of how myths are built. My father was a dynamic Episcopal clergyman. He was outspoken and controversial—qualities that always help myths develop.

In 2009 I went to Delaney Beach, Florida, for a retired clergy conference. When I walked in the door to register, two of the men at the registration table asked me if I was related to Ham Aulenbach. They wanted to ask me about an Easter story they had heard. In the story, my father was rolled into the center of the church in a coffin, and at a certain point in the service he raised the lid and shouted "He is risen."

I confessed that I had heard similar stories floating around but that none of them were true. I shared with them my idea of how that story might have started: Back in the 1930s when Dad went to a church that needed a "resurrection," he heard about another clergyman who went to a dying church and tried to revive it, but the people were just not responding. The pastor had a brilliant idea. He would have a "funeral" for the church and invite everyone to attend. On the Sunday morning of the funeral, the church was packed. The pastor read the service for the dead and then opened the lid of the coffin and invited the congregation to come forward and bid farewell to the church. All the people were curious about who would be in the coffin, so they lined up and passed by. One could see the shock on each face as the person gazed into the almost empty coffin. Why? Inside was a mirror where everyone could see his or her own face, intimating that the viewer was partially responsible for the death of this church. End of story.

When I told the two men the truth—that my father simply told a similar story—they seemed disappointed. Sometimes we prefer to believe in myths rather than accept reality. We gentiles who don't understand midrash insist on literal translations and often miss the main point.

The Magical Jesus

I know people who say that Jesus is their Christ because of all the magic he did. He is said to have walked on water, raised people from the dead, made a man born blind see with 20/20 vision, instantly cured a wild demoniac who had lived in a cave for years, cured a woman of a twelve-year menstrual problem with the simple touch of his garment, made extraordinary wine from water, taught fishermen how to catch nets full of fish, made a deaf mute hear and speak, and "unwound" the withered hand of a man. Some twenty-eight miracles are told in the canonical gospels.

I don't need or want a magician for a Christ. If I were looking for a miracle Christ, I might have looked to Kathryn Kuhlman (1907–1976), who flourished in Los Angeles as a faith healer with over seven hundred "healings" to her credit. (Unfortunately, someone spilled the beans about her so-called healings and almost put her out of business.) Kuhlman was a very colorful personality who began preaching in a Methodist church in Concordia, Missouri, at the age of fourteen. At sixteen, she switched to the Baptist church and as a young adult moved to Los Angeles to continue her rather lucrative business of healing.

The healing stories in the gospels are really a message wrapped inside a story. For instance, for a man born blind, being made to see as an adult is beyond a marvelous feat. It can't happen. Eyes not used for years are atrophied and useless. However, a person who has been a heavy user of drugs since adolescence, for example, can be considered "blind." If that person enrolls in a rehab program and makes the decision to stay sober, he or she is no longer "blind" but now metaphorically "sees" life through sobriety.

The Bizarre Jesus

I have met the bizarre Jesus in a variety of places. I mentioned the painting of Jesus as a white man with smooth skin and styled hair; I have also seen him portrayed as a baby sitting on his mother's lap, but he has a full beard and is wearing a crown on his head. He looks like an older child, not a newborn baby. And some people think a painting of Jesus having an uproarious, knee-slapping laugh is bizarre or even sacrilegious.

Then there are books about Jesus. I have one entitled *The Lost Books of the Bible*. The first work is called The Gospel of the Birth of Mary and claims to reveal almost all the intimate details of Mary's life and how she met Joseph.[1] The author plagiarizes some material from Matthew and Luke as he weaves a strange fantasy and makes Jesus sound like a spoiled brat whom I wouldn't want my son to play with.

Then we have "Thomas's Gospel of the Infancy of Jesus Christ." One of the more outlandish stories is about how Jesus, as a child, was playing with a neighborhood boy. The boy destroyed some fish pools Jesus had built. Jesus became angry and "withered the boy, all over." That must have been quite a sight! Needless to say, the boy's parents were furious; they marched over to Mary and Joseph's house and demanded that Jesus correct the withering, which Jesus did, "leaving only some small member continued to be withered, that they might take warning."[2] I'll let your imagination work on the "some small member."

One of my favorite bizarre books about Jesus is by Christopher Moore; it's called *Lamb: The Gospel according to Biff, Christ's Childhood Pal*. It's total fiction, but I think it is very funny. Some might say it is sacrilegious, blasphemous, and irresponsible—especially the part where Jesus got drunk at a party and barfed all over the donkey on which he was riding. Biff had to clean up the donkey while Jesus went into the house to sleep it off.

My least favorite bizarre reading is the book of Revelation, the last book in the New Testament. Revelation is a Gnostic interpretation that has next to nothing to do with the Jesus of the synoptic gospels—it's as if Revelation was written by a schizophrenic going through a psychotic episode. If that were the only book about the life of Jesus or Christianity, I wouldn't be a Christian.

The Combo Jesus

When people start combining the stories in the gospels, they are inventing a brand-new story that has no validity. Then they create the Combo Jesus.

Let me show you how this happens using the nativity story. Only two stories in the gospels are about the birth of Jesus, one from Matthew and one from Luke. The stories share hardly any similarities except for the characters of Jesus, Mary, and maybe Joseph, if he is a real person.

Matthew's story includes wise men who follow a star to look for Jesus. The actual story never says how many wise men there were, doesn't mention camels (in Turkey, they are shown riding horses), and doesn't say a word about a stable—in fact, they go to a "house," (Matt. 2:11).

Luke's long, elaborate story leads up to the actual birth in Bethlehem, where "there was no room for them in the inn . . . [so] they laid him in a manger" (Luke 2:7), but the story never mentions a stable. Then shepherds came and angels sang, but no wise men were there, and no one went to Egypt.

Combo stories take facts from each gospel, blend them, and add some details: for example, wise men and shepherds appear together. The Magi are numbered (three) and named in a hymn as Gasper, Melchior, and Balthasar. They are riding camels, and they all meet at a stable instead of a house, even though that never happens in the gospels. The wise men bring gold, frankincense, and myrrh. These three gifts were mentioned but not how many people were present—maybe fifty wise men saw the birth of Jesus. We have no idea.

Which Jesus do you like so far? If you said "none of the above," don't worry. We'll cover one more version of Jesus in the next chapter.

Nine Jesus Look-Alikes

Sometimes Christians think that Jesus was the only being who was ever born of a virgin, performed magic and miracles, died a cruel death, was resurrected, and rose to the heavens. He wasn't. He had many predecessors, and I would like to introduce you to nine of them.

The information in this section comes from a book written by Kersey Graves: *The World's Sixteen Crucified Saviors.*[3] I don't think you need to hear about all sixteen to get my point.

Let's start with Thulis or Zulis of Egypt, who went way back to 1700 BCE. He suffered a violent death, was buried, arose, and ascended to heaven, where he became the judge of the dead and of souls in their future state. Then he came down from heaven to benefit mankind as he was full of truth. This sounds a bit like the Nicene Creed, which came 2,100 years later.

Next, we have Tammuz of Mesopotamia, who flourished about 1200 BCE and was a god of Assyria, Babylonia, and Samaria, where he was known as Dumuzi. This god was an atonement offering, for salvation came out of his loins as he arose from the dead. Sound familiar?

Also in 1200 BCE was Crite of Chaldaea—another crucifixion victim—known as the Redeemer, the Ever-Blessed Son of God, the Savior of the Race, and the Atoning Offering for an Angry God. When he was offered up, both heaven and earth were shaken to their foundations. Why does this sound so familiar?

Then there is Hesus (sort of close to Jesus) of the Celtic Druids from the 850s BCE, who is depicted as being crucified with a lamb on one side and an elephant on the other. The lamb represents the innocence of the victim, while the elephant represents the magnitude of the sins of the world. Hesus was offered as a propitiatory sacrifice. All Anglicans say on a weekly basis that Jesus's sacrifice was "for the propitiation of our sins." I always loved to say that word—*propitiation*—it just rolls off the tongue, but its connotation seems rather savage.

In the early 700s BCE there was Indra of Tibet, who was nailed to a cross, with four wounds on his hands and feet and a piercing in his side. His mother was a virgin. He descended from heaven and then ascended back there after his crucifixion. He led a life of strict celibacy, walked on water and on air, could foretell future events with great accuracy, and was a god who had existed through all eternity.

Then around 600 BCE, Mithras of Persia was slain and crucified on a tree to atone for all mankind and to take away the sins of the world. Coincidentally, he was born on December 25.

Now let's go to Mexico around 580 BCE, where the god Quetzalcoatl (I can't wait to hear someone say it!) was crucified and nailed to a cross and is sometimes shown with two thieves hanging with him. If you have never heard that story before, see Luke 23:39–43.

Next we have Wittoba of the Telingonese who was around in the 550s BCE. To this day, he is represented with nail holes in his palms and his feet. His crucifixes are objects of adoration in the southern states of India.

Finally, we have Quirinius of Rome (not the one in the nativity story), who was conceived and born from a virgin around 500 BCE and then crucified, and at his death the whole earth was enveloped in darkness. He was then resurrected and ascended into heaven. I smell plagiarism.

Enough! When I went to seminary, no one ever suggested that Jesus had look-alikes, primarily because myth makers look at other myth makers to garner ideas, and it seems that virgin births, a nasty death, ascending or descending, and atoning for our bad behavior were great ways to beef up a story.

I'm sure you have seen my point without my having to describe the other seven saviors. The story of Jesus was told long before Jesus even showed up. None of the Jesus story is true as history, but the birth narrative and especially the story of Jesus's resurrection are powerful metaphors full of great truths. I share the above stories for the following reasons:

- Until I had read these "look-alike" stories, I thought Jesus was the only person who had ever done such unbelievable feats.

- I suspect the writers of the gospels had heard some of these stories and used the material to create their own stories.

- None of the heroes in the above stories are still around. But Jesus of Nazareth, whom some call their Christ, is very much alive. His name is a household word around the world, and people are spreading his message and doing projects to make this a better world in which to live.

I want to share some information about the birth narratives. They are metaphors.

I have always found it interesting that two of the major gospels, Mark and John, have no nativity story, nor does Paul allude to such an event. However, Matthew and Luke do, and these two writers spin nativity stories as different as night and day. Then one day I realized that both tales seem to relate to the political situation that existed when the gospels were written.

In both stories, Jesus is treated as royalty, as a very special person. Matthew features Magi who come from afar, follow a special star, are looking for the newborn king, and bring gifts one would present to royalty.

Matthew and Luke both say that Jesus was born in Bethlehem, the royal city of the great King David, with heavenly hosts making announcements, angels appearing, and shepherds recognizing this special birth.

Could this be the birth of the long-awaited Messiah who would free the people from the oppression of the Romans? The Roman Empire had an emperor (a god) with a huge army and sophisticated weaponry (for those days), and it conquered almost all of the Mediterranean basin by brute force, cruelty, and intimidation. That empire was full of corruption, intrigue, and the worst of humanity. That empire no longer exists.

On the other hand, Jesus's Followers (perhaps called Christians by then) had a leader, Jesus, recognized by some as a king (or perhaps the long-awaited Messiah) by the very intelligent and knowledgeable Magi, angels, heavenly hosts, a special star, and lowly shepherds, all orchestrated by NoOneUpThere.

This king, Jesus, had a vast army (Followers) who were conquering the world with one weapon: agape—unconditional love, total acceptance of all humanity, forgiveness of self and others, and love for "the least of these" (Matt. 25:45).

In my decades of ministry, it had never occurred to me that these two humanly impossible birth fabrications could be metaphors suggesting that the empire of agape and its king, Jesus, are much more powerful and long lasting than the Roman Empire and all its gods. Indeed, the Roman Empire is long gone, but the army of Jesus's Followers lives on, conquering the world with schools, colleges, hospitals, social service agencies, and ministries all in the name of this radical revolutionary Jewish peasant whose only weapon was agape.

The real message of the birth narratives has nothing to do with virgins, little babies, wise men, gifts, shepherds, or angels but is about the fact that some fifty to sixty years after the death of Jesus, the power of Jesus's message was finally recognized, and it still is.

The kingdom of agape is here and now, and everyone who wants to join is invited to enter the realm.

The Resurrection as a Metaphor

Early in my ministry, I taught that the resurrection was a real event and that Jesus wandered all around doing unbelievable things. In the back of my mind, I wasn't comfortable with this idea because it seemed to make Jesus into more of a first-century Houdini than a peaceful radical revolutionary.

As I wrestled with the concept of a physical resurrection, I had to take a hard look at my own death. What was there after this? Me shooting UpThere like a Gemini rocket was not the answer.

The story of the resurrection is a powerful metaphor. Let's try a midrash (an interpretation) of the story, starting with the idea that bad things happen to everyone. Some misfortune is caused by circumstances beyond our control, while other unfortunate events are caused by our own doing. Jesus had no control of what happened Thursday night and most of Friday after supper with his friends. For us, no matter how misfortune happens, we are all looking for a way to move through it. Some folks use drugs and the problem seems to go away—for the moment. Others try to ignore the event, hoping it will evaporate or pretending it didn't happen. Some become angry and start to place blame on everyone else. Still others exacerbate the problem by making another problem.

But what human beings want most is a way to move through the issue without suffering too much pain or causing too much damage. I see the idea of resurrection as the start of moving forward when bad things happen.

Let's go back to the events leading up to the murder of Jesus. The very short, painful process that Jesus went through when the soldiers arrested him until he was pronounced dead by the centurion is similar to what happens to us when life goes south. Pain and suffering are always involved—perhaps not quite as dramatic and painful as what happened to Jesus, but as we go through it, we know that it's hell on earth.

The church calls what happened to Jesus Good Friday, but I prefer to call it Bad Friday, especially for Jesus. The early church suggested that the unjust execution of a relatively young man is good for us because it is part of the salvific act planned by NoOneUp-There and would save us from our sins. But I don't believe that for a second. Jesus died because he was in the wrong place at the wrong time with the wrong message. Had there been a system of justice, Jesus might not have died. He would have been tried in a court of justice and set free to return to his preaching mission. Or had he decided not to go to Jerusalem, as a couple of his disciples had suggested, he would not have been crucified and would have continued preaching and teaching.

Back to the metaphor. We've established that every human being experiences misfortune, but how can we get through our bad days? Agape is the answer. By practicing agape, we can rise above all these negative experiences and keep moving in a positive, creative direction.

Let me share a couple of examples of how agape and the resurrection metaphor have helped me through hard times. The first is about my motorcycle accident.

In the hospital, the first thing I had to do was accept the painful fact that Brad was dead and no amount of blame was going to bring him back to life. Both Brad and I had purchased our motorcycles of our own free will. Both of us freely decided to drive to Tilden Park in Berkeley with me following Brad. NoOneUpThere had no involvement. The fire engine and firemen were simply doing their job. NoOneUpThere was not driving the fire truck or giving instructions to the driver to hit those two seminarians on their motorcycles. All of us were simply in the wrong place at the wrong time. I had to forgive the driver of the fire truck, even though he never forgave himself and died a broken man. I could not undo this. I had to move on. I had to ask for help. I had to think positively all the time, knowing that 90 percent of healing starts in the head. I had to show appreciation to the dozens of people who made good things happen during my recovery. I had to keep moving forward when things didn't go according to my schedule. I had to make this horrible event a positive in my life. I had to turn "bad" into "good."

When I graduated from seminary on time, I had to look at my recovery as being an Easter, or a resurrection experience. Had I turned negative, angry, or vengeful, I would have destroyed my life. But this was a resurrection experience and I still look at it as that.

I had the same reaction when our daughter Heidi was born with a multitude of challenges. I had to turn that "Bad Friday" into an Easter. "Poor Heidi, poor us" would have gotten us nowhere. Fifty years later, as we watch Heidi flourish in Seattle, we know that she has been an Easter experience, all centered on agape.

The metaphor of the resurrection is an extremely important part of my daily living. When I see a "Good Friday" happening, immediately I need to go into the resurrection mode by practicing agape.

When people die, we often feel their spirit, their message, and their way of living as if they were still alive. I still feel Brad's presence, even though he was killed almost sixty years ago. I am thoroughly convinced that Jesus was "resurrected" in the minds of his Followers when, after he had died, they felt his presence, heard his words in their heads, and put his wishes into action. They turned Bad Friday into Easter by keeping Jesus's teachings alive, acting out his message to love ourselves, our neighbors, and Creation.

Many present-day Followers still feel the presence, perhaps hear the voice, maybe even see an image of this man who was crucified some 1,800 years ago. I do. That's why the church is still here today.

When Did Jesus Become God?

Many people would answer the question "When did Jesus become God?" by saying "Jesus was always God. Period!" Sixty years ago, I also would never have thought to ask such a question. Thirty years ago, I might have imagined such a question but probably would have seen it as grounds for a heresy trial. But as I started to mature in my ministry, divorced the theistic god, and started seeing Jesus as a human, the question of when this quiet, revolutionary prophet was transformed into some kind of god became a pressing issue for me.

I searched Paul's letters, the earliest known writings; the so-called Q sources (a hypothetical source of the Gospels of Matthew and Luke); the Gospel of Mark, the earliest gospel; and even the Gospel of Thomas, which some think is even earlier than Mark, but I could not find a clear-cut, easy answer.

Then I heard of Dr. Bart Ehrman, a professor of religious studies at the University of North Carolina who wrote a book called *How Jesus Became God* and created a twenty-four-lecture series for the Great Courses with the same title.[4] Here's what I learned from his research: neither Jesus himself nor his disciples ever thought of him as God during his brief stay on earth. The best one could probably do was consider him a rabbi, a charismatic rabbi, who attracted large groups, mostly Jews, to hear him preach and teach. Above all, the Jewish hierarchy, as Jesus ranted against them, never saw him even as a rabbi, much less the Messiah or Yahweh.

The fact is, some powerful Jewish leaders accused him of claiming that he was "the King of the Jews." Then they told this to Pontius Pilate, and in less than twenty-four hours Jesus was dead. His close friends were caught off guard. Quickly, they dispersed and hid, fearing that they might be next.

Let's not forget that these disciples were primarily Jews awaiting the coming of the Messiah. I can easily understand how the disciples, seeing that the Romans weren't interested in pursuing them once their leader was dead, started thinking that perhaps Jesus was the long-awaited Messiah. His message was strong, powerful, and perhaps a bit apocalyptic. His Followers couldn't help but feel his messianic charisma.

This is where his Followers started bumping heads with the orthodox Jewish leadership, who had no interest in even considering Jesus as the Messiah. He didn't come close to matching their preconceived notion of the sort of person the Messiah needed to be.

But the Followers plowed ahead. The mood was right. The rebirth of Hellenism, where humans became gods and gods became humans, opened new doors. Also, in ancient Judaism, divine beings, sometimes called Angels of the Lord, came to earth in the shape of humans. Daniel 7:13 and the prophet Enoch mention that the "son of man," a name sometimes bestowed on Jesus, was a divine-sent human. Centuries before, some thought Moses to be the Messiah. Others saw King David as God or the Messiah.

At the time, the Jews were under an oppressive Roman occupation. The poor were becoming poorer and the rich richer. The future was bleak for most Jews. Even their own leadership was morally and financially corrupt. The people were desperately looking for and wanting a savior.

Jesus never called himself God in early writings, but he spoke a great deal about the Kingdom of God, which he suggested was here on earth. It was a utopian place that would free the people from oppression and give them new hope. Perhaps Jesus would lead the movement? His Followers felt he had the qualifications, but to further their claim that Jesus was the Messiah, a couple of negative issues had to be cleaned up. First, he died a criminal and his body was "cremated" in the city dump. That is not messianic material. So the Followers needed to develop some explanations to counteract the labels of *criminal, cremated, peasant,* and maybe *illegitimate.*

We never see a clear-cut statement suggesting that Jesus had been promoted to Messiah, but we do see some hints in Paul's first letter to the Thessalonians 1:1 (written about 50 CE), which referred to Jesus as "our Lord Jesus, God's Anointed" and "God's son from heaven whom God raised from among the dead, Jesus, who will rescue us from the condemnation that is sure to come" (1:16). This is only ten to fifteen years after Jesus was crucified. He seems to be on the promotion fast track. In 1 Thessalonians 5:10, Paul says, "God's Anointed who died for us so that . . . we might live together with him." That itinerant Jewish preacher, crucified as a criminal, no longer had a criminal record and had become a hero.

Three years later in his letter to the Galatians, Paul says, "Jesus loved me and gave up his life for my benefit" (2:20). In Galatians 4:4, he says, "God's son was sent into the world." Jesus's record is expunged in less than twenty years, and in Romans 1:4, Paul talks about Jesus's "resurrection from the dead," stating in 6:9 that Jesus is not going to die again: "death no longer has any power over him." We are now into dead-man-walking territory but don't really know the exact details of how we got here, except through fabricating details.

This is only a bird's-eye sketch of Professor Ehrman's thorough study, but from my vantage point, Paul has already almost deleted Jesus's basic message of agape and turned it into his own version of atonement theology.

The coronation of Jesus as God builds in the book of Mark, written around 70 CE as a collection of stories about Jesus. This gospel has no birth narrative—it starts with John the Baptist baptizing Jesus in the river Jordan. According to Mark's author, Jesus becomes God at this point. But also remember that the original Mark tells no resurrection story. It simply states, "He is not here" (Mark 16:6b). So we see no explanation about what happened after Jesus was executed. The resurrection story in Mark (16:9–20) is a redaction.

Matthew, on the other hand, explains quite a few things. In his genealogy, Matthew traces Jesus back to Abraham (the father of Judaism) but then tells a nativity story in which it is intimated that with the wise men coming, Jesus was more than any old baby being born into the world—he was Emmanuel, which means "God is with us." In about sixty years, Followers elevated Jesus from a preacher-teacher to the Messiah and finally to God who has been born into the world. The Followers of Jesus had been expelled from the religion of Judaism and had started a new religion almost entirely based on Judaism, except their God conquered death through his resurrection. The book of Matthew gives us the first description of how the resurrection happened.

Ten years later, the book of Luke traces Jesus's lineage back to the first human, Adam, and tells an elaborate nativity story about the birth of John the Baptist and the host of heavenly angels along with some humble shepherds coming to recognize the birth of "the Savior, the Anointed One, the Lord" (2:11). Luke's resurrection story is also more detailed, and he adds an ascension story to go with it.

The Gospel of John takes Jesus's promotion one step higher, suggesting that the "word" (Jesus) was there with God at the beginning. And a second-century group called Docetists, from the Greek word meaning "to appear" or "to seem," elevate Jesus further by stating that he wasn't really a human. He was God but pretended that he was human so all that crucifixion pain didn't hurt. That idea didn't go over very well, so the Docetists were condemned as heretics.

Let's jump to the third century and the Arian controversy led by Arius, a bishop of Libya who advocated that Jesus was subordinate to God and should be "demoted." Arius was condemned as a heretic but spent the rest of his life trying to defend his theory—but Jesus wasn't demoted.

Now the persecuted Christians have a huge break. Constantine, the emperor of the Holy Roman Empire, with his deeply religious mother's urging, made Christianity the major religion of his kingdom. One of the first things he had to do was to quell a heavy ecclesiastical controversy within the empire, so he called the Council of Nicaea in 325 CE. More than three hundred bishops attended, mostly from the eastern sector of the empire, and the majority agreed, after much discussion, that Jesus was the Son of God, which sort of makes him God—I think.

Dr. Ehrman ends his discussion here, but the church doesn't end its controversy about who Jesus was for a couple more centuries, so allow me to briefly fill you in as to how far the church took the "who is Jesus?" controversy.

The next controversy involved what was called Apollinarianism, after a man named Apollinarius, who advocated that Jesus had a human body and soul but he lacked manhood. In 382 CE, the Council of Constantinople decided that Apollinarius was wrong and that Jesus was completely, totally, and unequivocally human. I'm not sure if this was a promotion or demotion for Jesus.

Then in the fifth century, the Nestorian heresy evolved, which was opposed to the doctrine of incarnation and stated that God and Jesus were two separate persons. So the Council of Ephesus was called in 430 CE where it became official that Jesus was both fully divine and human. Whew! Finally, it's over!

But as Yogi Berra used to say, "It ain't over till it's over," and it wasn't over yet. A new controversy arose in 451 CE. The Council of Chalcedon was called, and it stated, in essence, "Enough is enough! This is it: Jesus is totally human and totally divine. There is only one substance but two natures." Then three more councils were held because in the church, enough is never enough. (I suspect you have had enough of this! I know I have.)

Well, maybe we could call one more council to resolve the heresy of "Bil-arianism," which states that Jesus was just as human as you and me and just as divine as you and me. The council will be held in 2017 at Irvine United Congregational Church and will be designated as the Council of Irvine. Religious leaders will be invited from all over the world to discuss the power of agape and Jesus will be demoted to a revolutionary prophet/sage who started a revolution, some two thousand years ago.

The Bible tells us to love our neighbors, and also to love our enemies; probably because they are generally the same people.
—G. K. Chesterton

CHAPTER 4

The Historical Jesus

We can only find out what life is all about when
we have the courage to do some of it differently.
—Sister Joan Chittister, *The Monastic Way*

I first heard about the historical Jesus—the real Jesus—back in the late 1980s when some friends shared with me the work of the Jesus Seminar, an arm of Westar Institute. The seminar tried to determine which sayings in the Bible Jesus may have really said and which were more likely the invention of others.

Unfortunately, we know next to nothing about the personal life of the man Jesus except that he was born a Jew and died one at the age of thirty or so when the Romans murdered him. We think his mother was named Mary, but we're suspicious about whether Joseph was a real person. We are rather certain that Jesus was an itinerant preacher, an advocate for the downtrodden, of peasant stock but charismatic. He was a thorn in the flesh to the Jewish hierarchy and a nuisance to the Romans who silenced him. Here are a few more facts we can use as a foundation for understanding who Jesus really was:

♦ The first written documents we have about Jesus are the seven authentic Pauline letters, the first of which could have been written ten to fifteen years after Jesus died. But it's obvious in those letters that Paul doesn't have a clue about the personal life of Jesus, or if he does, he doesn't share it.

- The church now has twenty-two different gospels, only four of which are in the Bible. Most of them are about what people thought Jesus said when he was alive. They shed very little light on the man Jesus, and except for the Gospel of Peter, none of them talk about a resurrection.

- The four gospels in the Bible were written forty to ninety years after Jesus's death, and each has its own bias.

- Many of the stories about Jesus came from an oral tradition, so the storyteller could have embellished them, forgotten some parts and made up his own, or deliberately changed them to suit his needs.

- The oldest New Testament manuscripts that scholars have to work with are from the third century, and some of those are in poor shape. The stories were originally told in Aramaic, Jesus's native language, and then written down and translated into Greek.

Meet the Real Paul

Paul is sometimes called the author of Christianity, and we know much more about Paul than about Jesus. Unfortunately, Paul's letters don't shed any light on the real Jesus. They are about his ideas of who Jesus was or should be.

Here are some of the things we know about Paul from his letters and the book of Acts:

- Paul's Jewish name was Saul. He was born a Jew, died a Jew, and did not start Christianity or have any idea what a Christian was. All his thinking was based on his strong Jewish faith and background.

- He was a rabbi like his father, who was trained by Pharisees and was also a famous teacher. Paul and his family lived in Tarsus (present-day Turkey), where his father purchased

Roman citizenship—this is how the Jewish Saul became the Roman Paul.

◆ After rabbinical school, Paul worked as an undercover agent to investigate that nuisance—Jesus—and his Followers, but Paul never suggests that he had seen or heard Jesus preach.

◆ Paul paints a very dramatic story about his conversion on the road to Damascus, but he had a tendency to exaggerate. He then had to lay low for about three years because the Pharisees considered him a turncoat and the Followers of Jesus didn't trust him. What Paul learned about Jesus was not from the lips of Jesus's close Followers but from hearsay—and we all know what that can do to facts!

Until about thirty years ago, most people believed that Paul had authored a total of fourteen letters. In the late twentieth century, however, scholars realized that seven of those letters—2 Thessalonians, Ephesians, Colossians, 1 and 2 Timothy, Titus, and Hebrews—are not from Paul, but many Christians still quote these books as if Paul wrote them. The authentic works of Paul are 1 Thessalonians, Galatians, 1 and 2 Corinthians, Philemon, Philippians, and Romans. Only these books can help us understand Paul.

In 1 Thessalonians, Paul suggests that Jesus was the promised Messiah, the Son of God, who would come in Paul's lifetime to usher in the Second Coming. When that didn't happen, Paul decided that Jesus's death on the cross was the new atonement and that God sacrificed his Son to save sinners. Within a year of writing 1 Thessalonians, Paul states, "He loved me and gave up his life for my benefit" (Gal. 3:20) and "I absolutely refuse to take pride in anything except the cross of our lord, Jesus, God's Anointed—the same cross that crucified this world for me and me for this world" (Gal. 6:14).

Obviously, Paul invented a Jesus who had little to do with the historical, human Jesus and his real message. I appreciate Paul's hard work and personal sacrifices to spread the idea that Jesus died for our sins, but two thousand years later, it's time to correct that erroneous idea and bring back the real Jesus and his message of agape, which Paul so clearly stated in 1 Corinthians 13:13: "Faith, hope, love abide, but the greatest of these is love, agape."

When people use Paul's antiquated first-century system of morality in the twenty-first century, they miss the main point of the gospels. Some of his wisdom may have been standard in the first century but is misogynistic today. For example, Paul states, "The wife does not have authority over her body, her husband does" (Phil. 2:12). My wife, our three daughters, our two granddaughters, and I don't believe this, even a smidgen.

Jesus and agape are the model for ethics, and Paul is not the spokesperson for Jesus. He's a short chapter in the history of the church. Leave him there.

The Gospels

In seminary, I learned that the books in the New Testament are not in chronological order, though many Christians believe that they are. Most people have no idea how the New Testament was formulated—that whoever compiled the Bible had so many manuscripts to choose from and that most of them appeared decades after Jesus died. A fight seems to be brewing between those who believe that some of these newer gospels should be canonized and those who believe the Bible should not be altered. I'll go with the first group because I think the church constantly needs to change with the times.

Many people are already familiar with the four gospels in the New Testament—Matthew, Mark, Luke, and John. Let's take a look at a few of the lesser-known gospels that didn't make it into the Bible. Many of these gospels are fragmentary, meaning that no complete copies exist—only fragments—so scholars have to guess what letters, words, or sentences are missing.

The Gospel of Thomas

The Gospel of Thomas is a collection of 104 supposed sayings of Jesus. Thomas's full name is Didymos Judas Thomas. *Didymos* means "twin," and some say Thomas was the twin brother of Jesus, but no evidence supports this idea. Scholars have known about the Gospel of Thomas for centuries but had no manuscript until 1945, when documents were found in the Nag Hammadi Library in Egypt. This gospel was written in Coptic and translated from the original Greek, so extensive research was needed to understand the documents. The best date we can give this manuscript is the latter half of the first century CE. Many of the sayings in Thomas are similar to those in the four New Testament Gospels.

The Secret Book of James

James is another book of sayings, and it suggests that 550 days after the resurrection, before Jesus's ascension, Jesus secretly shared a revelation to James and Peter. The book of James was written by someone with a wild imagination as late as the end of the second century—much later than 550 days after Jesus was crucified. James also contains Gnostic materials from the second and third centuries, when the church was well established. Reality is quite different from what this gospel says.

The Dialogue of the Savior

The next sayings gospel, the Dialogue of the Savior, was probably written about 150 CE. It is another finding from the Nag Hammadi Library but is from a fragmentary Coptic manuscript, which makes for interesting reading and heavy discussion among the translators and scholars. The author of this gospel deals with the afterlife as well as the necessity of baptism, primarily through a made-up dialogue among the Savior, his disciples, Mary of Magdala, and Judas Iscariot, the traitor long thought dead. This gospel could have been used as teaching material for catechumens, Christian converts, as they prepared for their rebirth through baptism.

The Gospel of Mary

Nothing is known about the origin or date of one of my favorite gospels, the Gospel of Mary—referring to Mary of Magdala. Only one copy exists, and a great deal of it is missing. This is a shame because I think it shares much about the importance of women in the early church. I suspect that some misogynist in the second century tried to rid the church of such a manuscript because early on, the institutional church wanted to restrict women to being property. A few verses in this gospel strongly suggest that Mary was the wife of Jesus. For instance, Peter tells Mary, "Sister, we know that the Savior loved you more than any other woman" (6:1), and Levi tells Peter that Jesus "knew her completely [and] loved her [steadfastly]" (10:10). What a game changer it would be if scholars found a document proving that Jesus was married to Mary of Magdala and that they had children.

The Gospel of Philip

Philip is thought to be from the third century and was also found in 1945 at the Nag Hammadi Library. Like the Gospel of Thomas, Philip was a fragmentary manuscript translated from Greek into Coptic. Verses 63:34–64:5 of this gospel support the idea that Mary of Magdala was married to Jesus. The author writes that "the Savior . . . loved her more than [all the] disciples [and used to] kiss her [often]. . . . They said to him, 'Why do you love her more than all of us?'"

The Gospel of Judas

Most Christians will tell you that Judas committed suicide after Jesus was arrested, but the Gospel of Judas doesn't even hint at that idea, focusing instead on Judas's role in the events leading to

Jesus's death. This story was probably written about 180 CE, first in Greek and then copied into Coptic. Only one fragmented manuscript exists, but it contains enough material to make this gospel very interesting reading, especially since it tells us about the twelve disciples when Judas was supposedly no longer among them.

Some scholars have suggested that Judas never existed and was "invented" for the purpose of validating a prophecy by Jeremiah, a seventh-century Old Testament prophet who said, "And they took the thirty silver coins, the price put on a man's head . . . and they donated it for the potter's field, as my Lord commanded." But this Old Testament quote is really from Zechariah 11:12–13, not Jeremiah. Matthew was a little confused as to who said what and when.

The Infancy Gospel of James

James was said to be the brother of Jesus who was a leader in the early Jesus movement, and his was the first infancy gospel—supposedly an eyewitness account of who Mary, his mother, really was. This gospel probably didn't show up until the second century, when all the eyewitnesses were long dead and gone. It's an elaborate story patterned after Luke's long and complicated nativity story where Jesus is God and Mary is the mother of God. The Greek word usually translated as "young woman" was interpreted as "a virgin of extraordinary purity and unending duration." One sees here the beginnings of the Virgin Mary cult and a whole new religion.

The Infancy Gospel of Thomas

Another finding from the Nag Hammadi Library, the Infancy Gospel of Thomas, has been dated from the late first to the second century CE. This one is a hoot! The stories show Jesus's development at the ages of five, eight, and twelve and portray him as a precocious spoiled brat who does awful things to his playmates, family, neighbors, and teachers. He also performs unbelievable miracles, such as instantly healing a young man who severed his foot while splitting wood. This gospel goes on for nineteen chapters, and each story is better than the last one. Late in the second century it was banned as heretical, but I certainly am glad that some insightful monk decided to save a copy. I love reading these fairy tales!

The Gospel of Peter

Peter is the only manuscript written in someone's cursive hand. This manuscript dates from the eighth or ninth century, but it must have been copied from a much older one. The storyteller is supposedly Jesus's close disciple Peter, and the story includes a more detailed narrative of what happened at the crucifixion, the burial, and the empty tomb than one will find in the four gospels. The Gospel of Peter is very short, and it ends abruptly with the idea that Jesus's tomb was empty after he died.

The Gospel of the Savior

This gospel features short collections of loosely connected sayings by the Savior (it never uses the terms *Jesus* or *Christ*), as well as a heavenly journey of the apostles in which they are transformed into spiritual bodies and a retelling of the passion story. Pieces of the manuscript were found in 1967 in the store of a Dutch antiquities dealer, and it dates from the latter half of the second century. I find it a strange gospel, very mystical and unrelated to the real Jesus. But I also feel that it should be included in the Bible so that people can see how the life-changing teachings of a Jewish prophet sage turned into an unbelievable fairy tale.

The Mystical Gospel of Mark

In the first quarter of the second century, the Mystical Gospel of Mark was widely circulated, but it was undiscovered until 1958, when it was found at the famous Mar Saba monastery near Jerusalem. It is about Mark, whom we know from the Gospel of Mark as the young man the centurions grabbed to carry the cross for

Jesus, who was having difficulty dragging it to the crucifixion site. The Mystical Gospel of Mark adds some very suggestive remarks to Mark's story: "The young man looked at Jesus, loved him, and began to beg him to be with him" (1:8) and, a few verses later, "He spent that night with him" (1:12). Then in 2:1 we find "The sister of the young man whom Jesus loved was there." Was this gospel suggesting that Jesus was gay or bisexual? We may never know.

Gospel Oxyrhynchus 840 and Gospel Oxyrhynchus 1224

Both Oxyrhynchus gospels are very short, and most of the latter is missing, forcing translators to conjecture as to what might have been written. The former was written on a single small piece of vellum measuring about two inches wide. It is rather graphic and depicts Jesus in a name-calling confrontation with the chief priest at the temple; Jesus says, "Damn the blind who won't see [referring to the Temple priests] . . . You wash and scrub the outer layer of the skin, just like prostitutes and flute girls . . . to entice men, while inside they are crawling with scorpions and filled with all sorts of corruption."

As you can see, we in the twenty-first century seem to have a great deal more material to deal with than in the past centuries. For me, the most interesting fact is that these gospels deal primarily with what Jesus said and don't mention "resurrection," leading me to believe even more strongly that the resurrection stories are metaphors and not the literal truth. It is also interesting to me that Jesus seemed to have much more than a casual interest in Mary of Magdala. I think she was his wife. If that was proven to be true, what would that do to your thinking?

These are just a few of the gospels. More probably remain to be discovered, but none of them tell us who the man Jesus was; they just offer lots of conjecture about what he might have said. All the conflicting information and wild stories in these gospels provide a convincing argument that the church needs to reexamine its creeds, its dogma, its doctrine, and its theology and make them relevant to the twenty-first century. We can start that process by reconnecting with the real Jesus.

The Real or Historical Jesus

The idea of Jesus as a real human being did not exist during my childhood, in seminary, or in the early years of my ministry. I was looking for him but had no idea how to find him. Then in 1985, a Biblical scholar and avant-garde thinker named Robert Funk, along with other like-minded folks, started the Westar Institute and developed the Jesus Seminar as a segment of Westar. The seminar attracted over two hundred scholars whose objective was to create, from the gospels and other writings, an image of the real Jesus.

The Jesus Seminar's methodology involved scholars going over every saying, parable, and sentence in the gospels, studying it in detail, and discussing it thoroughly before voting on its authenticity. If they voted "black," that meant Jesus did not say those words. Rather, someone else in the early church interjected material that he thought Jesus needed to say. A vote of "gray" indicated that Jesus did not say the words, but the idea might be close to what Jesus might have said. "Pink" meant Jesus could very well have said something like this but not using this exact phraseology. And "red" signified that Jesus undoubtedly said this or something very close to it. In 1999, the Jesus Seminar published the book *The Gospel of Jesus: According to the Jesus Seminar.*[1] This book has become very controversial, and some biblical scholars don't subscribe to this sort of scholarship.

At this stage in my life, I feel that I have a clear idea of who Jesus was, what he said, and what he wants his Followers to do. I also think that it is helpful that Annie and I have visited the Holy Lands; walked the narrow cobbled streets of Jerusalem; traveled along the hot, dusty roads; felt that desert sun; seen Nazareth and parts of Galilee; mingled among the crowds; visited the market-places; and seen so many of the historical sites, some real and others imagined. That trip has been a huge help in allowing me to envision this Jesus doing his daily life and carrying out his ministry.

What historical facts do we absolutely know about Jesus from the four gospels and some of the letters of Paul? Next to none. We know he was born around 4 BCE; had an active ministry, mostly in Galilee; and was crucified. But to see a bigger picture of the real Jesus, we must use a process called *Sitz im leben*, a German phrase meaning "the situation in life." In this process, we go to real history books and see what was happening with the Romans, the Herodians, the Jews, Galilee, and the Temple. From there we can build a visual scene and then place Jesus in that scenario.

Let's try an example. Although nothing in the New Testament tells us specifically how Jesus traveled from point A to point B, we know he did not use a car, bus, train, or plane. I suspect that he did not ride any sort of animal or go in a cart because that would have been too slow. The only alternative left is walking, sometimes for long distances, up and down mountains, on hot, dusty, lonely roads. Now envision that Middle Eastern Jewish man, with a covering over his head and a white tunic, walking on those roads for days at a time with some of his friends. Maybe they are talking or, as they climb up steep mountains, they are quiet. I can see and feel this Jesus in my mind very clearly.

To meet the real Jesus, we have to keep doing this envisioning process. In the rest of this section we're going to try to do just that, using what facts we know.

The Romans occupied the part of the world where Jesus lived. Caesar Augustus was emperor from 30 BCE until 14 CE, and Tiberius was emperor from 14 to 37 CE. During the lifetime of Jesus, the empire was rather peaceful and featured an excellent road system, primarily designed to move soldiers and equipment quickly from one area to the next.

Despite the relative peace and safety, the Jews hated the occupation. I suspect that Jesus also disliked the Romans. Why wouldn't he? No one likes to be occupied and especially by those who had total disregard for one's religion and way of life. Common people were badly overtaxed by the Romans, Herodians, and Jewish leadership. Roman culture, language, customs, and mores seemed to permeate every facet of their Jewish life. Jesus and his Followers must have felt the spread of Hellenism, especially when the Hebrew scriptures were translated into Greek, and Hebrew became a dying language.

Herod the Great ruled from 47 BCE until 4 BCE and was designated "King of the Jews" by the Romans, even though he was not considered Jewish by most Jews. Herod was appointed to collect taxes and keep the peace. He overtaxed his subjects but, on the other hand, was a great builder who provided all sorts of employment on his many projects. When he died in 4 BCE (about the time that Jesus was born), his youngest son, Herod Antipas, took over—after murders, banishments, and jockeying for position within his family. He too was a builder (he rebuilt the Temple in 18 CE) and a heavy taxer, as was his brother Philip, who ruled the area including Galilee, where Jesus performed a great deal of his ministry. Philip had a much better reputation than his brother Herod Antipas but was still a good friend of the Romans.

In 26 CE, under the reign of Emperor Tiberius, a procurator (a financial and military leader directly responsible to the emperor) was appointed governor over Judea. His name was Pontius Pilate and he lasted ten years. He was popular with no one but ruled with an iron fist.

When we take the time to understand what was happening in the world of Jesus when he was alive, we can better understand why Jesus might have said or done what he did.

Matthew suggests that Jesus was born in Bethlehem, King David's city and the home of the future Messiah, but Matthew seems more interested in conforming to a prophecy than in telling historical facts. Luke also has Jesus born in Bethlehem but says he was living in Nazareth. Scholars now believe that Jesus was born and raised and centered his ministry in Galilee.

Some archaeologists question whether Nazareth even existed in the time of Jesus. So far, we have no evidence to prove that it did. We'll assume that it existed but was very small and stayed that way until the fourth century, when Emperor Constantine recognized it as the birthplace of Jesus. Then it started to grow. Today it's a booming metropolis (dealing primarily in tourism) of about seventy thousand people, almost everyone an Arab Muslim.

Luke 2:21–52 tells a story about Jesus's circumcision when he was eight days old and then his presentation in the Temple in Jerusalem. It's a nice story, but Jerusalem was a long, hard trip up the mountains from Nazareth, and it was an expensive city in which to stay. Jesus's family was poor and couldn't afford the time or money to make that journey and pay all sorts of taxes and temple fees for a simple presentation. This story is better viewed as a myth developed to fulfill some Old Testament prophecies.

The reality is that Jesus lived in a small village, probably with other Jewish families. I suspect the village had a small synagogue that was the center of Jewish life and would teach the boys scripture, maybe a little Hebrew, and some Greek from the Septuagint (Old Testament). Jesus and the other students were taught by an elder who might not have had much book learning himself. Once Jesus learned to walk and talk, he became a helper, first to his mother and then, about the age of five, to his father by beginning to learn carpentry skills. Matthew 13:55 states that Jesus's father was a carpenter, and speculators suggest that he made wooden farm implements. In the real world of Jesus, a son had to learn his family's trade so that he could carry on the business if anything happened that made his father unable to work.

Annie and I visited a small town in Israel where the residents still speak Aramaic and not much had changed in two thousand years. A group of boys was playing in the street. I could "see" Jesus there playing with his friends, very animatedly saying all sorts of things we couldn't understand.

At about twelve, Jesus would have become a bar mitzvah (a son of the law) and been recognized as a Jewish male adult. At some stage, I suspect that Jesus wanted to satisfy his religious thirst, but we have no idea what Jesus did for the next sixteen years. Rumors suggest that he went to India to study, and some Indians claim to know exactly when he lived there and under whom he studied. Another rumor placed him in the cloistered order of the Essenes, a rather austere group whose members kept to themselves, had strict adherence to the law, studied Jewish scriptures, and forbade sex, which eventually resulted in their demise.

According to Matthew (13:55) and Mark (6:3), Jesus had brothers and sisters. No one is certain if these were children by a previous marriage of Joseph's, if Mary gave birth to all of them, or if they could be the figments of someone's imagination. The boys' names were James (who later became prominent in the early church), Judas, Simon, and either Joseph (Matt. 13:55) or Joses (Mark 6:3). The gospels refer to sisters but give no names; after all, women were only property and treated poorly. When they became of age, women were "sold" for a dowry to be cooks, maids, and baby machines to their new owners, also called husbands.

My conjecture about what happened to Jesus during the lost sixteen years (ages thirteen to twenty-nine) is that Jesus left home to join a group such as the Essenes, saw the futility of being cloistered, and struck out on his own as an itinerant preacher. It's obvious that Jesus was very Jewish, practiced his faith, knew Jewish scripture, was challenged by the direction he saw Judaism going (loving the law and not people), and felt he could make a difference as he tried to push his agenda. He must have been a charismatic preacher to be able to pull together and surround himself with such a close group of diverse people: fishermen, tax collectors, businessmen, and an entourage of women. His message had the power to attract hundreds to come hear him.

At some point, Jesus set up his "headquarters" in Capernaum, a large, very important city on the north shore of the Sea of Galilee. Jesus is reported to have journeyed as far north as Tyre, not too far east of the Sea of Galilee, west to the seaport town of Caesarea Philippi, and south to Jerusalem, Bethany, and maybe Bethlehem, but most of his active ministry was spent in Galilee.

Galilee is reported to have had about 240 small villages in Jesus's time, whose inhabitants were primarily farmers. Most of the commercial life in Galilee was centered on the Sea of Galilee, a thirteen-by-seven-mile lake that was a trade center. Not only was fishing a big industry but wine, olives, grain, and cattle were also very important businesses.

Some of Jesus's closest Followers were fishermen who fished the Sea of Galilee, mostly at night. If the wind was blowing, they could use a sail to move their boats; otherwise, they rowed their boats to the fishing area. Once they arrived at the fishing spot, dropped their nets, and hopefully had their catch, they had to pull in the heavy nets, row back to their base, and spend the day repairing their nets and boats. Alternatively, they could drop the nets in the evening, go back to shore, and then pull in the nets with their catch at the crack of dawn.

In 2006, Annie and I visited Vietnam and were staying at China Beach, a beautiful, expansive beach north of Da Nang. We were taking an early morning walk on the beach when we noticed a group of Vietnamese fishermen and their families pulling in a net from the ocean. Two groups about two hundred yards apart were working together. Jokingly, one of the fishermen motioned for us to come and help. They had about six people on each end, so we took them up on their offer. We grabbed the rope, dug our feet into the sand, and helped them pull. Then we repositioned ourselves and pulled some more. We thought that net had to be full of huge fish. Finally, after about half an hour the net was in. We were soaking wet from sweat, our hands were blistered, and there were no more than fifty small fish in the net. This experience gave me some insight into what the fishing life was like in the time of Jesus.

What might Jesus have looked like? Based on the appearance of people who live near Galilee today, one might say that Jesus was dark skinned, had long dark hair and a beard (a religious convention), was slim, and looked like a Middle Eastern Jew. I suspect that he wore the ordinary clothing of the day, an undergarment and a tunic.

From Jesus's reported actions and reactions in the gospels, I envision a man with a good sense of humor. In the gospels, Jesus told funny stories, but we do not necessarily see them as funny because they are not our brand of humor. For example, the story about Jesus casting a demonic spirit into a large herd of pigs strikes us as mean spirited and would give PETA a fit, but a herd of two thousand pigs running down a hill and over a cliff and drowning in the sea (Mark 5:1–20, Matthew 8:28–34, Luke 8:26–39) would be a very funny image to a group of Jews who considered pork dirty and prohibited their Followers from eating it.

Jesus also had his bad moments. Every once in a while, we see his anger, indignation, impatience, and short fuse. Much of this negativity was directed at the religious leadership, but Peter, James, and John, to name a few, were also recipients. If one reads Matthew 23, one sees Jesus's blatant hostility toward the Pharisees. Early in his ministry, he appeared to be hostile to gentiles (anyone who was not a Jew) but later in the gospels I feel he changed his tune and became much more accepting. I can see his prejudices ooze out when he deals with rich people, Samaritans, most gentiles, bad bosses, and cheats.

When people suggest that Jesus was "perfect" (there is no such thing, except in the eye of the beholder), I want to suggest that they have not read the gospels in any depth. Jesus was a fellow human being with all the same weaknesses that you and I have. I love his humanity. I identify with it easily.

At times, I feel Jesus used bad judgment. Against the advice of his friends, he went to Jerusalem, and that was the end of him. He had to know that many of the Pharisees and scribes did not like him and wanted him out of the way. He must have known what they did to John the Baptist for speaking out. Why wouldn't they do that to him?

Had he not ventured to the Holy City, he might have lived a very long life as a prophet and sage. But of course, this always brings up an interesting question: Had he lived to be an old man simply preaching and teaching, would the world have heard of him? It has been suggested that his premature death and martyrdom at a young age is what caught the attention of people in the rest of the world who loved his message of agape.

Jesus's practice of agape led him to associate with many kinds of people who were shunned by Jewish society at the time, such as lepers, tax collectors, mentally ill and disabled people, women of ill repute, and menstruating women. Another disparaged group was the Samaritans, who claimed to be the Chosen People, remnants of the kingdom of Israel from the tribes of Ephraim and Manasseh. The Samaritans built their own temple and had their own laws and beliefs, which were very different from other Jews'.

Jesus must have rubbed some of his people the wrong way when he told the story of the good Samaritan, in which a Jewish priest and a Levite were the bad guys and the Samaritan the hero. The Gospel of John (4:1–42) includes another story about Jesus and his disciples passing through Samaritan territory and speaking with a single woman, a Samaritan one at that, who was alone and had a questionable reputation—a "no-no" for orthodox Jews. It seems as if Jesus did a series of things that alienated the Jewish hierarchy. He told negative stories about the leadership. He publicly flouted the law in front of the authorities. Matthew 23 contains a long list of Jesus's name-calling aimed at the scribes and Pharisees. Sometimes one has to wonder if Jesus was deliberately alienating himself from the higher-ups. Wasn't he smart enough to realize that the opposition would tolerate only so much abuse before they pounced?

In this book, I give readers a bird's-eye view of what life was like when Jesus was alive. Volumes of books are available that will help one develop a bigger and more thorough picture of what daily life was like in the time of Jesus, which then gives one an opportunity to see who Jesus really was and why he might have done and said what he did. I've listed a few of my favorites in the "Additional Resources" section at the back of the book.

Despite these prejudices and setbacks, Jesus continued to preach his message of agape and invite his Followers to create the Kingdom of God on earth. This is the real Jesus, and he is my Christ—not because the Bible, religious authorities, or my parents said I have to follow him but because when I rejected the myths and met Jesus as a real, historical human being, I knew I had found someone who could give me the tools to live life to the fullest and be a messenger of peace, love, joy, and hope.

> *A generous heart, kind speech, and a life of service and compassion are the things which renew humanity.*
> —Buddhist teaching

CHAPTER 5

My Marching Orders

If you want others to be happy, practice compassion.
If you want to be happy, practice compassion.
—Dalai Lama

It was 1956. I was a second lieutenant in the Marine Corps, stationed in Hawai'i. We were making landings on a remote beach on Kaua'i, later to be a missile site. I was in charge of a platoon of forty-four men and twelve amphibious tanks, which could "swim" in water and drive on land. I landed the troops and had the tanks deploy them to what I thought were strategic spots. I had no orders—I never did on these maneuvers. After a year or so of working without orders, we had a new commanding officer, who became very irritated that I wasn't deployed where I should have been. I told him I had no orders, but he didn't believe it.

Then I found out why I never had orders.

We had just finished a week of landing troops on Maui. A small boat pulled up to the landing ship, asking for Lieutenant Aulenbach. It was Naval Intelligence. I went with the officers to their headquarters in Honolulu, where they told me that I was being charged as a Communist spy for three reasons:

1. My father was a Communist. This was in the McCarthy era, when so many were suspected of being "Commies." Later I found out that my father was accused of being one because he had once given a dollar to a Communist front organization, thinking it was an agency against drafting men in peacetime.

2. I had "stolen" confidential maps of a future missile site and given them to a Communist in Japan. (I had thrown the maps away. They were not marked "Top Secret.")

3. I had met with a card-carrying Communist in Japan. In reality, I was friends in college with a Japanese man, a Christian, assigned to be a kamikaze pilot in World War II. Peter had been lined up for three missions, but none of his airplanes worked properly and he survived the war. When I was stationed in Japan, Peter and I partied. Naval Intelligence was following us. The story goes that after the war, Peter ate free lunches at the Communist Party headquarters on his university's campus. (He never joined.)

When Naval Intelligence finished with me, I went home, called my father, and shared the story. He was furious! Being a lifelong patriot, World War I veteran, and Republican, my dad had no qualms about calling President Eisenhower, but he ended up talking with Vice President Nixon. I suspect Nixon heard an earful. Within ten days I had a note of apology from the Marine Corps commandant and Top Secret clearance. That was the end of my being a Commie, and from that point on I knew what to do when on maneuvers.

My point in sharing this story is that without the right tools—marching orders—I felt like a ship without a rudder, always drifting.

I see people drifting in their daily lives with no marching orders. I watch folks feeling obligated to go to church but having little or no idea what Jesus wants them to do to live life to the fullest.

In the Marine Corps, I realized I needed marching orders to be effective. But as a layperson, I found that the church did not help me. I had to be baptized, go to church, and give money, and the rest was supposed to fall into place. It didn't. In seminary, I started to find my marching orders, but it took me quite a few years in the ministry to figure them out. In retrospect, the marching orders were obvious and readily available to everyone who simply read the Bible. They weren't secret, and no one needed clearance, but I never had clergy nor laity point the way to me.

The foundation stones of my marching orders are Jesus's references to the Old Testament. First, he quotes the book of Deuteronomy: "You shall love the Lord your God with all your heart, and all your soul, and with all your mind, and with all your strength" (6:30). Then he quotes Leviticus: "You shall love your neighbor as yourself" (19:18). Then the teacher says, "There is no other commandment greater than these" (Mark 12:31).

Here is my interpretation. First and foremost, it's very important for me to love myself, not in a conceited way but in acknowledging that I am a creature of Creation, warts and all. As a part of Creation, I have to love myself. I need to know myself, my strengths, and my weaknesses. I need to keep strengthening my weaknesses and using my strengths to make this a better world in which to live.

Because I love myself, in the best sense of that word, I can now love "my neighbor" (every other human being on earth) more fully without allowing my biases and prejudices to dictate whom I want to love. I also know that I don't have to like everyone and everyone doesn't have to like me, but I do have to respond in a positive, creative way to everyone.

The importance of loving Creation and loving our neighbors as well as ourselves is evident in Jesus's powerful phrase "On these two commandments depend all the law and the prophets" (Matt. 22:40). In other words, as Followers, if we are able to strictly adhere to the principle of agape, then we would no longer need the law or more prophets.

This may sound utopian and impossible to achieve, but if we all were to strive toward this goal of love, far fewer problems would trouble the world today. I also know that I have become a much better person in the process of trying to achieve this utopian goal.

Of course, we still need "the law of the land" to give people guidelines on how to live together peacefully, but we also must understand that some of the laws of the land that are passed are not always just and loving. As Followers, we must fight those laws in the name of agape.

Now that I've laid down my foundation stones, let's look at more marching orders. A saying that helps me monitor my use of judgment is from the three synoptic gospels, Matthew, Mark, and Luke. I'll quote Luke's version: "Why do you notice the sliver in your friend's eye but overlook the timber in yours? You phony, first take the timber out of your own eye and then you'll be well enough to remove the sliver in your friend's eye" (6:42). In other words, as soon as I'm perfect (and there is no such thing), then I can start working on the imperfections of others. This can be very difficult in a marriage. One of my favorite cartoons shows a pastor in front of a couple being married, saying to the groom, "This union is now the end of you being your own best self-critic."

When I find myself being critical or judgmental, I have to remind myself of my own prejudices and biases. Is my judgment based on my hang-ups or on an unbiased point of view? Too often, it is based on my prejudices. I need to keep working on that sliver in my own eye.

Another passage I use a great deal is in I Corinthians. It is called the love letter, and I often read it at baptisms, confirmations, weddings, anniversaries, birthdays, and funerals because it is so powerful and expresses very clearly the essence of agape: "Love is patient; love is kind; love is not envious or boastful or arrogant or rude. It does not insist on its own way; it is not irritable or resentful; it does not rejoice in wrongdoing but rejoices in the truth. It bears all things, believes all things, hopes all things, endures all things. . . . And now faith, hope, and love abide, these three; and the greatest of these is love" (13:4–13). This passage hits the nail on the head—the most important message is agape.

No aspect of agape is easy, but some of Jesus's sayings help me exercise forgiveness of both myself and others. I suspect that the lack of forgiveness is one of the biggest hindrances in our quest to achieve world peace. For example, as I write this, the Armenians are once again bemoaning the fact that the Turks will not apologize for the atrocities that happened a hundred years ago. By refusing to forgive the Turks and move on, the Armenians continually remind themselves of how awful the situation was—a hundred years ago. No one and no institution can move forward when they keep dragging the past with them. I hear Jesus very clearly telling me that I have to forgive, as do the Armenians, if I want to live life to the fullest.

In the Gospel of Matthew, Peter asks Jesus, "How many times should I forgive a person? Seven?" (18:21). Jesus then replies, "No, seventy times seven" (18:22). Seventy times seven is 490, a Jewish number meaning "infinity." The Orthodox Armenian Church needs to take this to heart and urge people to move on to bigger and better things, such as relieving poverty and dealing with issues in their own country.

Jesus wants us to love even our enemies. He says, "You have heard that it was said, 'You shall love your neighbor but hate your enemies.' But I say to you, love your enemies, pray for those who persecute you" (Matt. 7:43–44). We also find marching orders in Matthew to "turn the other cheek" (5:28–42), and in Luke we find "If someone takes away your coat, give them your tunic also" and "Love your enemies and do good and lend expecting nothing in return" (6:29–30).

I find that the faster I can forgive myself and others, the faster I can creatively move on with life. I love this story about the family of Amy Biehl: Amy, a graduate of Stanford University, was an attractive, young, vibrant volunteer working for a worthy cause in South Africa. She was murdered by a group of black men, reportedly because she was white. Her four murderers were caught, tried, and sentenced to prison for a long time. But Amy's parents, instead of seeking vengeance, decided it would be best for all to forgive these young men and allow them to move forward with their lives. Two of the four men are now traveling around the world sharing the power of forgiveness.[1]

The most powerful message Jesus gives us is found in Matthew, "The Last Judgment." In this story, the reader is taken into the next world and told about how people will be separated the way a farmer separates sheep from goats. The teller, a king (the Son of Man or perhaps Jesus), then suggests that when he was hungry, thirsty, naked, sick, and in prison, people cared for him. The listeners in the story are surprised because they hadn't made any of those caring gestures to him. He then suggests, "Truly, I tell you, as you did it to one of the least of these who are members of my family, you did it to me" (25:40).

My main mission in life is to serve others, including my wife, our children, our family, and my neighbors—in the larger sense of the word. The main mission of Jesus's Followers, and the institutional church, should be to serve, not build buildings, develop liturgies, exclude anyone, amass large amounts of money and things, save themselves, or otherwise serve their own self-interests. Followers must go into the world and love the "lepers" of today's society—the homeless, the elderly, the developmentally or physically disabled, those addicted to anything, deportees, the poor, runaways, those starving to death, the incarcerated, veterans, and so on. This is what Followers do. Serving is our primary job and can be done in a myriad of ways from just giving a smile to going out to the mission field for long periods of time.

I have many more marching orders, but I'll end with one from Luke (17:21b) and Thomas (3:1–3). Some Pharisees were speaking with Jesus and one of them asks, "When will the Kingdom of God come?" Jesus responds, "On the contrary, the Kingdom of God is among you. The Kingdom is inside you and outside you." The idea of the Kingdom of God or agape is not pie-in-the-sky fantasy. This is it. This is not a dress rehearsal. We have to live life to its fullest here and now.

The Man and His Message

If I could ask Jesus to describe his ethical system, I fantasize that he would say something like this: "I'm a Jew, and I live under the Jewish law—all 613 laws. The Torah guides me. But we Jews became so busy following the letter of the law that we lost our way. So, I went back to our roots, the book of Deuteronomy, and reminded my disciples that we are to love God with all our hearts, all our souls, and all our might. Then I reminded them that Leviticus instructs us to love our neighbors as ourselves. These two commandments have replaced all the laws and the prophets. Together they are the Great Commandment. Follow the Great Commandment and you'll have a rich, full life."

In his book *Beside Still Waters*, Gregg Easterbrook writes: "Such was his gift that Jesus simplified the entire structure of spirituality into a single sentence. 'This is my commandment, that you love one another as I have loved you.' . . . The Commandments have fallen from Ten . . . to One and encountering the One Commandment we find the focus entirely on the human."[2] Easterbrook then boils it down even more, pointing out that the phrase "God is love" can be found in some form in the writings of every faith.[3] Amen!

The phrase "God is love" has the power to change individuals, institutions, and the world—as long as we understand the meaning of the word *love*. In the English language, only one word signifies the concept of love. So we hear people saying that they love their significant other, their pet, God, their car, their parents, ice cream, wine, or a movie. In each case, they use the same word, so we have no way of knowing the intensity of that person's feelings unless we ask.

The major language of the early New Testament writing was Greek, even though this was not the primary language of Jesus. He probably spoke Aramaic, a Semitic dialect related to Hebrew. Perhaps Jesus knew a few Greek words and phrases, but Greek was the language of the Roman conquerors, and most Jewish people disliked using it. I suspect Jesus also knew some Hebrew, but in his lifetime, the Old Testament (the Septuagint) had been translated into Greek and was usually read in the Greek language during worship.

We shall look to the Greek language for our study of the word *love*. The Greeks have four different words for love, each signifying a different meaning and intensity.

The most common Greek word for love is *philia*, and it represents the kind of feeling that exists between casual friends, neighbors, or people with whom we work. It's a reciprocal relationship but without much intensity—if one person moved or died, the other's disappointment would be short-lived.

The next level of love is *storge*, and the word represents familial love, the feeling that exists between siblings or with one's parents or relatives. We might fight like cats and dogs with our family members, but we're quick to defend them if they're being mistreated.

The third level of love is *eros*, erotic love. This love occurs between people who have a reciprocal sexual relationship.

The fourth and highest kind of love is very different from the first three. The Greek word for it is *agape*, and this love is the foundation stone for Jesus's ethics. The first major characteristic is that this love is given freely, unconditionally, with no strings attached. The giver does not expect anything in return, and if he or she receives something, that's just a bonus. Another major component of agape is total acceptance of everyone. That includes mass murderers, sexual predators, ISIS—everyone. This requisite is extremely difficult to fulfill. Too many institutionalized religions have their lists of people who cannot be loved. Some are long, some written, some unwritten. Jesus says over and over, and I paraphrase, "No lists! My kingdom of agape is for everyone." (One of my favorite examples of this is in the Gospel of John where Jesus is speaking with the Samaritan woman at the well. He accepts her as she is: a Samaritan, a woman, perhaps with a questionable past, who has had five husbands. All these traits would be negatives in Judaism and would disqualify her from being a card-carrying Jewess.)

One of my favorite nuns is Sister Helen Prejean, a Roman Catholic sister who spreads agape as she befriends some of the most horrendous people in the world on death row. Her book *Dead Man Walking* was made into a movie starring Susan Sarandon and Sean Penn. Sister Helen accepts death-row inmates as they are and treats them with love and respect. Most of society considers death-row inmates to be throwaway people, but the message of agape is that no such concept exists—Creation is within us all.

Another favorite agape story is about Leonard Beerman, a dynamic, outspoken, courageous rabbi who recently died at the age of ninety-three. In 2014, on Yom Kippur (the holiest day of the year for Jews) in a packed temple, he said this to his congregation: "Another Yom Kippur. Another 500 children of Gaza killed by the Israel Defense Forces, with callous disregard for their lives." He continued: "Hardly a word found its way out of a Jewish mouth to express the slightest concern about the way Israel was exercising its right to defend itself, the appalling human suffering." The consequences of his brave statement could have been the nation of Israel blackballing him, his synagogue firing him, or members taking their money and leaving. But no one walked out that day. Rabbi Beerman was not afraid to share a painful truth in the name of agape.[4]

Another cornerstone of agape is forgiveness, given to all—always. Jesus tells us to forgive seventy-times-seven times, which correlates to an infinite number. In 2015, a neo-Nazi walked into a Bible study in a black church in the South and executed nine people, but within thirty-six hours, the family members had forgiven the murderer.[5] They wouldn't forget what he did—their forgiveness did not negate how drastically this tragedy would change their lives, and it did not suggest that he shouldn't pay for his actions. But they didn't want to carry a hatred within themselves that would eventually destroy them. The family members of the victims truly understood forgiveness in the name of agape.

The final component of agape is that of putting love into action. Most of us care about many things. We can spend our lives caring, but that in itself doesn't cause anything to happen.

Let me pick on the Episcopal church. It's the only denomination with which I am thoroughly familiar. Every time we do the Eucharist, we repeat "The Prayers of the People" and ask the Lord to have mercy on a long list: our bishops and all the clergy; the leaders of nations; our city; seasonable weather; all who travel on land, water, or in the air; the aged and infirmed; the widowed and orphaned; the sick and suffering; the poor and oppressed; the unemployed; the destitute; prisoners and captives; all who have died—and the list goes on. My problem is that each week, we tell NoOneUpThere what to do, until we return the next week and can remind NoOneUpThere what jobs to do again.

It would be much more effective to have the priest assign each of the above demands to a member of the congregation and then have everyone report back the next week on what he or she has done to fix the issue. I suspect we would stop using that useless prayer very quickly. To truly carry out Jesus's message, we human beings need to put agape into action.

The Ethics of a Progressive Follower

In 1966, Reverend Canon Dr. Joseph Fletcher, professor of social ethics at the Episcopal Theological School in Cambridge, Massachusetts, published the book *Situation Ethics*.[6] It caused a firestorm, primarily because it introduced a new way of thinking—and too many church folks don't like new. I bought it and couldn't put it down. I have read it at least ten times and have taught classes about the concept.

As I read the New Testament, I often envision Jesus using Situation Ethics. For instance, Jewish law forbids people to make contact with lepers—they must never touch them or even allow them to live in their cities. Jesus couldn't have cared less about what the law said in this case. He befriended the lepers and would do the same with the hated tax collectors, the enemy Samaritans, the adulteresses, and anyone else who was on the Jewish list of undesirables.

Here are the five basic standards on which Situation Ethics is built:

1. Only one thing is right and good: agape, the deepest love there is.

2. Agape includes total acceptance of oneself and all other human beings, whether we like them or not.

3. We must genuinely forgive ourselves and others immediately rather than blame, look for a scapegoat, or harbor grudges. One of my favorite sayings is "Resentment is like drinking poison and waiting for it to kill the enemy."

4. Every ethical decision is different and needs to be made based on the circumstances, not on a law or rule.

5. Only the end justifies the means, nothing else. Agape is always the end.

Situation Ethics is not for people who like to conform to a definite structure or strictly follow rules and laws. But if people or institutions can be flexible and sometimes go against the rules or traditions, then situation ethics could be their cup of tea.

When I first went into the ministry, I could see no logical reason why a divorced person could not be remarried in the church. The institutional church said, "Absolutely not!" But I married divorced people anyway. Forbidding remarriage was not a rule based on agape. Some years later, the Episcopal church said, "Okay, you can marry them, but only if the divorced people are willing to hang out all their dirty laundry and tell the juicy details of their divorce." Is that forgiveness or judgment? I know this: agape had nothing to do with that requirement.

What I like most about Situation Ethics is that the only definite factor is agape. The final decision depends solely on the circumstances, which differ in each situation. A great example of this is the story of a woman who committed adultery in the name of agape. Some folks might say that the church would never condone adultery for any reason. I disagree. So does Situation Ethics. It all depends on the circumstances.

I borrowed this example from Dr. Fletcher's book. Let me share it with you in my own words.

During World War II, a Soviet military unit captured a woman, Mrs. Bergmeier, who was digging through trash cans to find food for her three children. Unable to send word to her family, she was taken to a prison camp in Ukraine.

Her husband had been captured in the Battle of the Bulge and taken to a prisoner-of-war camp. When he was released and returned to Berlin, he spent weeks rounding up his children. His wife's whereabouts remained a mystery, but he and their children never stopped searching.

Meanwhile, in Ukraine, a sympathetic commandant told Mrs. Bergmeier that her husband and children were trying to find her. But Soviet rules allowed him to release her for only two reasons:

illness needing medical attention beyond the camp's capabilities, in which case she would be sent to a Soviet hospital, or pregnancy, in which case she would be returned to Germany as a liability.

She mulled over her situation and finally asked a friendly guard to impregnate her, and he agreed. Mrs. Bergmeier knew that she was committing adultery, a grave sin in the eyes of society, and to make matters worse, her newborn child would be labeled a bastard. But her act cannot be taken lightly, as if she was just feeling lustful in prison camp. Once her condition was medically verified, Mrs. Bergmeier was sent back to her family in Berlin. They welcomed her with open arms, even after she told them how she managed to arrange it. When the child was born, they loved him with the view that little Dietrich had done more for them than anyone else.[7]

Too many Christian churches would have condemned Mrs. Bergmeier, the guard who impregnated her, and perhaps even Dietrich, refusing to baptize him, believing him unfit to be a child of God. Some believe that adultery is evil regardless of the circumstances. I, however, think Mrs. Bergmeier was a courageous woman who put her family's needs above all else in the name of agape. In my eyes, she's a hero because she did the most loving thing a mother could do for her family, and one couldn't ask for a better ending. I am grateful to Situation Ethics for teaching me to put circumstances, people, and love above the law.

The Power of the Real Jesus

Annie and I have traveled extensively to sixty-seven different countries in our fifty-five-plus years together. Everywhere we go we see Jesus's "businesses" flourishing, even in Communist countries and countries where Islam flourishes. Followers have founded schools for local children, children with disabilities, and orphaned children; colleges and universities; and hospitals. In south Orange County, California, at least five hospitals are founded in Jesus's name. In this same region, one can find Christian drug rehabilitation centers, social services agencies, senior citizen housing, jail visitation programs, organizations that provide food and shelter for the homeless, and food distribution centers, among many other businesses started by Followers.

When I was a young priest in Hawai'i working with youth, I saw a great need for a runaway shelter. I shared that need with my bishop, who liked the idea and happened to have an empty house that could be put to such use. We took that need and our empty house to the Honolulu Junior League, which grabbed the bull by the horns and opened the shelter within six months. That was back in the late 1960s, and in 2016 the agency that operates the shelter, Hale Kipa, is still flourishing, with a multimillion-dollar budget and a large dedicated staff on every island. Hale Kipa is a pioneer in rescuing and working with at-risk children and adolescents to make them responsible citizens.

Here's another example. We travel to Mexico frequently to visit some of our projects, and on one of these trips we visited a shelter in Tijuana called Casa del Pobre. The shelter was run by seven nuns from the Philippines who came to this border city to start an agency with no money, only the desire to help "the least of these." The shelter now has facilities for free medical care (provided by volunteer doctors from both sides of the border), free medicines, free lunch for hundreds of people, free used clothing, free shelter from the dangerous streets, and many other free services for the needy.

Jesus was murdered almost two thousand years ago, but the power of his message and his life lives on. I identify with Jesus as a fellow human being who has been through some rather rough situations. He knows how life can be, with some good days and some not so good. Let me give you some examples. My family lived through the Great Depression. It was not easy. Jesus was born into poverty. Jesus experienced alienation from family members, a few of whom wanted to stone him to death. In my family, we experienced a horrendous lawsuit from a sibling that kept the family divided for years. The Jewish religious establishment, for the most part, made Jesus's life miserable. They were always on his case. I was fired from two churches because another clergyperson didn't like what I was doing and saying. The Jewish hierarchy did terrible things to Jesus, and some people in my church's hierarchy have made my life miserable. I could go on with our similarities, but that's not my point. I simply want to say that Jesus has given me the tools I need to move through similar situations that he had, and these tools, all based on agape, are powerful.

One day at IUCC, we were talking about modern prophetic voices and discussing Dr. Martin Luther King, Jr. He is one of my heroes. When he was marching for civil rights, we lived in Hawai'i and I couldn't raise enough money to fly east and join his movement. I often wonder what life in the United States, and the world, would be like if Dr. King had lived on. *The Radical King* includes a speech Dr. King made at the annual Southern Leadership Conference on August 16, 1967. It was his last speech to this group, and people felt King was extremely radical.

Dr. King spoke about all the murders of innocent blacks and all the police brutality. He was suggesting how difficult it was not to retaliate with murders and brutality, but then he stated, "You can't murder hate through violence. Darkness cannot put out darkness; only light can do that. And I say to you, I have decided also to stick with love, for I know that love is ultimately the only answer to mankind's problems. . . . I'm not talking about emotional bosh. . . . I'm talking about a strong, demanding love. . . . If you are seeking the highest good, I think you can find it through love. . . . John was right, God is love."[8] We need more Martin Luther Kings who not only discuss what needs to be done but also are willing to do the groundwork to make it happen.

Over the years, I have read lots of information telling me that Jesus was an apocalyptic prophet advocating the Second Coming. I don't buy into the idea that this was his mission, but I understand why so many poor, oppressed people might feel that way. If I was under all that oppression and didn't see any light on the horizon, I too would be advocating for change. When I see our sense of morality spiraling downward, our politicians dumbing down, and our idea of democracy becoming convoluted and favoring the rich, I too sometimes wish for a Second Coming in the form of new, moral, ethical leadership. But this isn't going to happen. What *can* happen is that each person makes the necessary changes in his or her life. Some people who have made such changes call this their second coming.

My understanding of Jesus's apocalyptic sayings means that the Second Coming happens when we practice agape. We are "born again" when we begin using the power of agape in our daily lives, and the Holy Spirit is that Creative force within each human being. These are my foundation stones. Each of us is capable of enacting powerful change in our own lives when we practice Jesus's powerful message of agape—loving Creation, our neighbors, and ourselves, as well as forgiving those who have mistreated us and taking action to help those in need.

> *I believe in the religion of Love,*
> *Whatever direction its caravans may take,*
> *For Love is my religion and my faith.*
> —Ibn Arabi

PART III

FIXING THE

BROKEN CHURCH

CHAPTER 6

How to Fix the Broken Church

*The biggest men and women with the biggest ideas
can be shot down by the smallest men and women with
the smallest minds. Think big anyway.*
—Kent M. Keith, "The Paradoxical Commandments"

When I started in the ministry in 1960, the church was alive and a vital part of our society. New churches were being built, people were filling them, seminaries were full of men (sorry, no women yet), and Pope John XXIII was leading his church out of the fourth century and into the twentieth.

Then fundamentalism started to flourish and aimed to be a power that took over our country. Megachurches began springing up, and quantity became more important than quality. Churches starting splitting apart because the liturgy was changing. Women were being accepted into the ministry, and gays and lesbians came out and wanted to be ordained. Inner-city churches were being closed. Families became so busy with activities for their children that Sunday morning became their only time off. "Spiritual but not religious" (meaning "I love God and nature, but I don't need the institution") became a new category on religious preference lists. No one seemed to care if people belonged or even went to a church or not.

It is blatantly obvious to me, a clergyperson on the sidelines, that the institutional church is dying and rigor mortis is setting in. Too many church folks are *not* accepting that reality.

I think the church can be fixed, but only if it wants to be. Some churches seem to be happy with the status quo, and others would rather die than change. Some of the steps to fix the church must be radical, maybe even painful.

- ◆ Step One: Verify that all those involved—individual churches, their congregations, and church leaders—even want to change. Clergy must be prepared to take risks that could be detrimental to their careers.

- ◆ Step Two: Bring in outside consultants who can be objective in unearthing problems and developing creative solutions.

- ◆ Step Three: Don't close inner-city churches. Reinvent them to provide the kinds of services needed by the people who live nearby.

- ◆ Step Four: Make new church building projects interdenominational and interfaith ventures to foster cooperation and understanding across religious traditions, as well as to save money and ensure that the buildings are used much more extensively.

- ◆ Step Five: Shift the role of seminaries so that they are leaders of the future, not purveyors of the past.

- ◆ Step Six: Hire trained teachers and use modern, relatable materials in children's and youth programs, and foster meaningful dialogue in adult programming with an interfaith focus.

- ◆ Step Seven: Constantly promote the idea that the interfaith community needs to work together to address social issues and engage in outreach programs to the less fortunate.

One of the biggest problems in mainstream churches is that the same irrelevant dogma and doctrine that was taught hundreds of years ago is still taught today. The world has transformed radically in my lifetime, whereas the church has hardly changed. Most of our seminaries are Followers of the old ways and are not seen as beacons of light to lead the church forward. We need seminaries to blaze a new trail.

Denominational seminaries need to join forces to develop interdenominational seminaries so that churches can build bridges instead of walls between fellow Christians. Seminarians should be encouraged to develop interfaith relationships as well.

One of the opportunities that was neglected in my seminary training was learning about the Jewish Jesus rather than the Christian Jesus. To be prepared for preaching and teaching, I needed to learn about Jewish customs and law, midrash, the Talmud, and the Hebrew language. I think I would have developed a deeper appreciation of Jesus earlier in my career had I explored his Jewish roots in seminary and been in contact with Jewish people.

These kinds of interfaith relationships are beneficial not just for religious scholars but also for the world. Interdenominational and interfaith cooperation can be a formidable force for change when one is working on issues such as poverty, fair wages, our unjust justice system, racism, overpopulation, and climate change.

Another way seminaries can progress is by training seminarians in financial matters. The church is a big business. When I directed the Episcopal camps in Hawai'i, I developed programs, hired qualified staff, and kept the camping experience fun and interesting. All of this cost a great deal of money, but I was never trained in high finance. I pleaded with the diocesan treasurer to take over the financial aspects of diocesan camping, but he refused, leaving my financial records unprofessional and wide open to abuse.

The church faces lots of controversy today, and seminaries need to teach conflict management and arbitration skills so that churches don't fall apart due to internal spats or dissatisfaction with the clergy. The average stay in the ministry for new pastors seems to be about five years due to problems ranging from a poor selection process and poor training, to unmet salary expectations and burnout. In my experience, one needs about ten years of on-the-job training to figure out what ministry is all about, so to have clergy drop out after five years is a waste of time and money. We need to find creative ways to address this problem so that the church will continue to have seasoned clergy leading their congregations forward.

You might think that all these steps for fixing the church seem utopian or unattainable, but I don't feel that way. I think Christianity has a most viable product, as do other religions. Jesus's message is still inspiring people and institutions two thousand years after the messenger's death—that alone should give us hope. Annie and I belong to a church that has already made several of the above-mentioned changes, so I don't see fixing the broken institutional church as impossible. On the contrary, I see it as very doable, and in the next sections I'll share more ideas about how to make it happen.

Searching for Sunday

A couple of times a year, IUCC invites outside speakers to discuss stimulating subjects. One such speaker was Rachel Held Evans, a bright young woman in her thirties whose blog has over eighty thousand Followers. Rachel came from a staunch fundamentalist background before matriculating into the Episcopal church. When she began thinking about what her fundamentalist church was saying, doing, and teaching, it didn't make sense to her. She began to see how fundamentalism was permeating every facet of her life, her thinking, her politics, even her friends, making her feel more like a puppet than a thinking person. Rachel did not want to grow up to have such limited thinking.

In her book *Searching for Sunday*, Rachel discusses why millennials are leaving the church: "We're tired of culture wars, tired of Christianity getting entangled with party politics and power. . . .

We long for our churches to be safe places to doubt, to ask questions, and to tell the truth, even when it's uncomfortable. We want to talk about the tough stuff—biblical interpretation, religious pluralism, sexuality, racial reconciliation, and social justice—but without predetermined conclusions or simplistic answers."[1]

In one of her question-and-answer sessions at IUCC, she was asked how churches can attract young people when they seem to be so busy with everything else. She emphasized that the most important thing to do is to tell the truth about our outdated dogma, doctrine, theology, and traditions. The church can be so defensive about dealing creatively with its irrelevant belief systems, and many young people don't trust what the institutional church believes.

One of the more interesting ideas that Rachel presented was that millennials don't like church buildings, which make them feel hemmed in both literally and figuratively. She shared a story about a bar where young people liked to go to socialize and sing hymns because bars have an open and free quality unlike the trapped feeling that church buildings can inspire.

Rachel's main message was that if the institutional church wants to remain relevant in the future, it needs to look very hard at how to attract young people. The church must learn to take a vastly different approach. As she writes in her book, young Followers of Jesus "can't be won back with hipper worship bands, fancy coffee shops, or pastors who wear skinny jeans."[2]

The Lord's Prayer—Sort Of

Back in the early 1970s, the Episcopal church was trying to bring its outdated liturgy into the late twentieth century, daring to change the wording of the Lord's Prayer to be more like the ones we find in Matthew and Luke. This change almost started a revolution in the pews—many in the church wanted to retain the old, phony version of the Lord's Prayer rather than use the newer yet more authentic one. Once more, tradition overruled authenticity. The church backed off very quickly, and we returned to using the old version.

I know that I am playing with fire, but I'd like to suggest a major revision to the Lord's Prayer. In this rendition, there is NoOneUpThere to give commands to or beg favors from. I've renamed it the Jesus Prayer. (Remember, the word *Lord* has feudal connotations.)

> Our Creation, which is in the entire Universe,
> Holy is your name.
> Our Kin-dom come. May agape be done on earth as in all Creation.
> May we share our daily bread.
> As we forgive ourselves, so may we forgive others.
> May we not be tempted by temptations but have the will to confront evil.
> For here is the Kin-dom, the power of agape, and Creation's glory.
> So Be It!

This new version could use some improvements, but I like that it has the same cadence of the Lord's Prayer we use today. Small changes in the words make big changes in meaning. In this version, we are not telling NoOneUpThere what or what not to do. We have promoted God to Creation—a force that exists throughout the universe. Most importantly, we are reminding ourselves what we have to do on a daily basis.

I am only a bit player in this effort to make the church relevant in the twenty-first century, and in the vast array of what needs to be changed, the "fix" of this revised prayer is miniscule. But it does demonstrate that bidding adieu to the theistic god in our prayers, hymns, and homilies is not that difficult. We can still pray and sing hymns without having to cave in to a theistic god.

Churches That Came Back against All Odds

At lunch one day, our pastor shared with me that IUCC had been featured in Paul Nixon's book *We Refused to Lead a Dying Church* in a chapter called The Progressive Alternative Church.[3] I wanted to share a few other examples of progressive churches that are creatively solving the problems of institutional churches, not only to attract new members and pledges, but also to be a force within their communities.

Portland, Maine, is the home of one of these churches, called HopeGateWay. At one time, it was a powerful, wealthy, well-attended church that had lost its way and become a small, ineffective, downtown disaster. Then a new leader persuaded the few remaining members to sell the church and use the proceeds to reinvent itself. They joined forces with a synagogue and purchased not a church but an office space. In it they built large meeting rooms, a well-equipped kitchen, a gift shop, a gathering area, and a children's area.

Then the members began reaching out to become part of their new community. They started the Wayside Food Kitchen, which served more than eight thousand meals in its first year, and sponsored all sorts of community activities.[4] Too many downtown churches simply close their doors and miss the opportunity to be an enriching part of their changing communities by offering ministries that are relevant to the people who live or work there.

I like this example because first, the church sold its property, which had too much tradition attached to it. The old-timers were hanging on to that tradition instead of moving forward. Then the church joined forces with a synagogue, emphasizing the need to work with the interfaith community. Next, they bought a space that did not look like a church and did their ministry from that non-threatening place. Together, the church and the synagogue identified the needs of their community and responded accordingly. I think Jesus would have been very happy with their direction.

Nixon's book includes fifteen stories of churches that carried out innovative projects to fix their congregations. These stories share a few commonalities, and each of these commonalities has at least one simple solution as spelled out below:

- ◆ Older clergy have a tendency to stay around too long, resisting change and preventing younger clergy from bringing in fresh ideas. One simple solution is to limit how long a clergyperson can stay in one position. This used to be standard practice. Each clergyperson can think of only so many creative ways to run his or her church. After ten or fifteen years, not much new happens, and too many leaders become complacent. Complacency is a church killer!

- ◆ Many churches seem to be clubs for like-minded people who only pretend to welcome everyone. One simple solution is to pursue a designation given by the United Church of Christ called Open and Affirming. Churches earn this designation by adhering to a high set of standards—it cannot be obtained by simply applying. IUCC is an Open and Affirming church, and I think this status should be a prerequisite for churches of the future.

- ◆ If a church loses members and is on the brink of going under, the property is sold, which halts that church's influence on its community. One simple solution is for that church to thoroughly study the ways it could stay relevant to its neighborhood and carry out these ideas by seeking funding from secular or philanthropic groups and joining forces with other churches facing similar challenges.

In Portland, Oregon, the Montavilla United Methodist Church was in decline as incomes dropped and crime increased in its formerly middle-class neighborhood. Then the situation began turning around when a new pastor, a woman, opened the church's doors first to a young Hispanic congregation and then to another church group from Tonga. The church became known as the unofficial community center, housing food ministries, a meeting place for the neighborhood association, a liturgical dance group, a community choir and orchestra, art shows, a creative writing group, a couple of book clubs, an annual poetry event, the Filipino cultural center, and groups such as the Council for Prostitution Alternatives. By responding to the needs of its community, the church was able to survive and thrive.[5]

My last example takes us to Washington, DC, where a synagogue fell apart after a Jewish flight to the suburbs. The synagogue was sold, and the area became depressed, but later it became valuable downtown property. The former synagogue went up for sale again, and three private developers (all Jewish) decided they wanted the presence of Judaism there, so they bought the property and developed it into an interfaith, interdenominational community center. I love their mission statement: "Where Jewish identity and community intersect."[6]

The innovative, reimagined community center became an integral part of the community by welcoming all people, regardless of their faith or beliefs. This story shows that three private developers knew that the presence of a faith-based organization was extremely important to the growth of this community. This center could be a model for communities of the future—interfaith, interdenominational, inclusive, Open and Affirming, and honoring of the diversity of the community.

From Seminary to the Pulpit

Barry E Blood, Sr., a retired aerospace manager and lay minister who has a passion for the study of religion, wrote a book called *Giving Voice to the Silent Pulpit*. His main thesis is that what is taught in academia and seminary is vastly different from the thinking in the pews. He asks why. Does the church feel that people in the pews can't handle this sort of information? What would or could happen if regular people in the pews were exposed to the theology of progressive Christianity? Would the church split and die?

It's time that the clergy level the playing field and start to share academic information with the congregants. Yes, some folks might leave, but maybe some new people might come or dropouts might return. The people in the pews need to hear fresh progressive thinking that comes from highly regarded scholars who have much more interest in sharing the truth about our beginnings than in perpetuating the many mistruths about Christianity.

Blood's book includes ten examples of well-known church doctrines, comparing their academic interpretation to what people think they mean. In the book's final example, Blood summarizes people's beliefs about life after death: "If you believe that Jesus is the Son of the living God and repent of your sins, when you die you will live in heaven for eternity. Those who do not believe and do not repent will spend eternity in hell." He contrasts this with the academic perspective: "The concept of a life after death based on a reward/punishment philosophy existed prior to the forming of Christianity. It is a behavior-control tool used to control the masses and to provide hope in the face of finite mortality. There is no literal heaven or hell to which humans ascend or descend after death."[7]

Have you ever heard the academic idea preached in church? I suspect not, but the concepts of heaven and hell are still going strong. Unless we dispense with the outdated idea of a theistic god and all its surrounding mythology, the survival of the institutional church is at risk.

Wake us from our slumber of indifference,
open our eyes to their suffering and free us from the
insensitivity born of worldly comfort and self-centeredness.
—Pope Francis, from a memorial service for
asylum seekers in Germany

CHAPTER 7

"Why Christianity Must Change or Die"

Exploration is the nature of the human mind. Not to feed it new sights, new ideas, new people, new questions, new challenges is to starve the soul of its potential to be stretched. It shrivels us up before our time. It deprives the world of our perceptions just when the world needs them most.
—Sister Joan Chittister, *The Monastic Way*

This chapter's title is also the title of a book, but better yet, it's an extremely provocative statement.

When I graduated from seminary in 1960, the church was alive and well, a powerful, highly respected force in our country. Seminaries were full, new churches were being built, and on Sunday mornings the pews were filled with people from every generation.

What happened? Can the downward slide be slowed down?

I know someone who can give us some answers: the Right Reverend John S. Spong, the retired Bishop of the Diocese of Newark and a dedicated Follower of Jesus who has seriously impacted the Episcopal church and the world. Not only is he a prolific writer with a deep understanding of the church, but he also practices what he preaches. Because of Spong's bold stands, women and members of the LGBTQ community have been ordained in the Episcopal church. If the church had dozens of bishops like Spong, I probably wouldn't be writing this book because the work I'm doing now would have already been done. History will remember him as a major mover and shaker of twentieth and twenty-first-century church and its theology.

Bishop Spong issues a weekly newsletter, and in the December 2015 edition he began a new series called Charting a New Reformation. As an introduction to part one of his series, he writes, "On October 31, 1517, so the story goes, a solitary monk named Martin Luther approached the great doors of All Saints' Church in Wittenberg, Germany, on which he planned to post a document entitled 'The Dispute over the Power and Efficiency of Indulgences.' History has renamed it 'The 95 Theses.' It was designed to call the Christian Church into debate."[1]

Near the end of the introduction, he writes that his series will build on Martin Luther's 95 Theses by questioning "the substance of Christianity itself." Spong questions whether the ideas of God, the creeds, the ultimate truth, an infallible Pope, and an inerrant Bible still have relevance today, and he puts forth twelve new theses on the topics of God, Jesus, original sin, the virgin birth, Jesus as the worker of miracles, atonement theology, the resurrection, the ascension of Jesus, ethics, prayer, life after death, and judgment and discrimination. Bishop Spong anticipated taking three or four weeks to go over each thesis in his newsletter, and his entire list of theses took nearly a year to cover.[2]

The bishop has stated that these are ideas for discussion, not an ultimatum. He presents the facts as he sees them, hoping that his readers, progressive clergy, and seminarians will read, study, discuss, and share this sort of thinking. Bishop Spong's theses could be the foundation stones for building the reformed church.

In Spong's book *Why Christianity Must Change or Die*, he discusses his ideas for the future of the institutional church. He does not deal with the structure, authority, or hierarchy of the church but rather with its theology, liturgy, and sacraments. Discussing what a new kind of worship might look like, he writes, "Both the liturgy and the structure of that emerging Church will have a very different look—so different, in fact, that I wonder if we will see continuity between the Church of yesterday and the Church of tomorrow."[3] He goes on to speculate that the reimagined church "will create new architectural forms, new organizational structures, and new identifying marks."[4]

I have no doubt that churches would look quite different if we were to promote the theistic god of today's church to be the God of all Creation and make the theological changes suggested in Spong's twelve theses, such as treating the "virgin" birth as a mistranslation of a word that originally meant "young woman," reworking our interpretation of miraculous stories, and using prayer as a reminder for ourselves rather than a to-do list for NoOneUpThere.

I also have no doubt that if our churches keep promoting the same-old-same-old-same, they are doomed to failure. For evidence, look at some of the churches in Europe, most of which are dying or dead. One percent of the population uses those huge, expensive, antiquated buildings that, for me, are simply tombs to honor their dead theistic god.

But on a positive note, if progressive churches and seminaries continue striving toward being interfaith, interdenominational, inclusive, and Open and Affirming, and if they continue to explore new ideas for attracting young people and integrating with their communities, a reinvention of our churches and a return to Jesus's message of agape is within our reach.

Jesus Is a Verb, Not a Noun

In the early fall of 2015, Annie and I were in Ecuador, in the historical city of Cuenca, studying Spanish in the morning and working in an orphanage for boys in the afternoon.

Almost every Spanish tutor I've ever had has told me right off the bat, "I don't discuss religion or politics." But often the very next thing we do is talk about religion. Once they learn that I am a progressive Episcopal priest, they want to talk.

My Spanish tutor for this trip was a father of two teenagers who taught in a technology school and tutored Spanish students in the mornings. He was a committed Roman Catholic who belonged to an RC men's group that was built on the premise of serving others. He shared with me his belief that the name *Jesus* is a verb—an action verb that steers him in every facet of his life.

He found a recording on the Internet of a Spanish song that represents this idea: "Jesus Verbo No Sustantivo," or "Jesus is a verb, not a noun." What a powerful notion: the action words of Jesus are going to make our world better. I've always liked the analogy of Jesus as a head and his Followers as a body: the hands and feet of the Followers carry out the work of Jesus's ideas.

Jesus instructs us to *visit* prisoners, *feed* the hungry, *clothe* the naked, go into the world and *teach*, *serve* those who are less fortunate than us, and to *practice* agape every day. By carrying out these action verbs, we can create the Kingdom of God on earth.

Stop Cramming: Start Living!

A friend of mine once asked me why I write books. The short answer is that I like to be provocative—I want people to think about what they believe or don't believe. I appreciate it when lecturers, authors, and scholars challenge my thinking. I love to sit around with a group of people and exchange ideas about anything and everything. In my twenty-five total years of education, for the most part I was taught to think, ask hard questions, and make up my own mind.

My entire ministry has been focused on challenging people's thinking—not to suggest that their thinking is wrong and mine right but to encourage them to look at life in shades of gray instead of black and white. Over the years, I have discovered that many people don't know how to think outside the box, perhaps because they feel they aren't allowed to or will be punished for doing so. The Episcopal church tolerates a bit of thinking, as long as that thinking stays within certain parameters. Getting rid of a theistic god seems to be outside those acceptable parameters.

Some folks like the process of hearing different ideas, but other folks don't want me to mess with their thinking. Their Sunday-school theology has worked for them all these years, so any new ideas could undermine their whole way of doing life. My intention is never to offend, only to stretch minds—including my own. In journaling about my faith journey, I feel that I was able to stretch my mind to see where I was, where I am now, and where I want to go.

My thinking has changed radically over my eighty-five years. To this day, much of what the church teaches makes no sense to me. But within those teachings are great truths and invaluable guidance for living. Reaching those truths has required me to ask tough questions. Another reason I write books is to let people know that I—a man of the cloth, a minister, a priest in the Episcopal church—am asking some of the same hard questions they are. I want this book to give my readers permission to think way outside the box and ask difficult questions while still being part of a faith-based community.

After my motorcycle accident, when the priest asked me what Brad and I had done to deserve God's punishment, I knew I needed to reexamine my faith and open my mind to new theological possibilities. First, I had to reject the idea of NoOneUpThere before I could do more progressive thinking. That was not easy. Second, I had to stop receiving a paycheck or the church would have fired me for my heretical thinking. Third, I had to slowly work through the tremendous transition of overhauling my belief system. It wasn't going to happen overnight. As soon as I began to work through this transition, a whole new world opened to me, a world built on reality and truth.

When I deposed the theistic god and began thinking about the idea of Creation, a universal force, I was able to come to these conclusions:

- Jesus is not the son of NoOneUpThere, and his divinity is the same divinity that you and I have as creatures of Creation.

- The Bible was written by human beings.

- The birth narratives in Matthew and Luke are metaphors.

- Virgin birth, immaculate conception, and other myths surrounding Mary are just that: myths.

- Jesus was an excellent teacher and preacher, but he was human and had his own weaknesses and imperfections.

- Jesus died on a cross as a criminal, and his body was burned in the city dump, making the resurrection stories a metaphor—but an excellent one.

- No Second Coming or Apocalypse will happen. Nor is there an antichrist. And the book of Revelation could be accurately classified as first-century science fiction.

- We must use midrash to understand the truths within the miracle stories in the gospels.

- Heaven, hell, and purgatory are not actual places but states of being.

- There is no divine plan, and each of us must be fully responsible for ourselves.

- The Holy Spirit is not a ghost but a spirit of agape that resides in every human being.

- The Kingdom of God is not an event in the future but is created here and now when Followers practice agape.

- Prayer is a reminder of what we must do, not a demand telling NoOneUpThere what to do.

◆ With the outdated dogma and doctrine out of the way, we can easily understand what Jesus wants us to do to make the world a better place.

When I make statements like these, many people ask, "Is Bil Aulenbach even a Christian?" As a Follower of Jesus—meaning the real, historical, human Jesus—I consider myself a Christian, but if I were to be tested by the institutional church's dogma and doctrine expert, I suspect I would fail the test—badly.

Does that bother me? Not necessarily. Part of me often wonders if I want to be called a Christian. The Christian church certainly has had a checkered past. Some of its history makes ISIS look like choirboys. On the other hand, the world is full of wonderful examples of the excellent work the church is capable of, especially in troubled areas of the globe. In our travels, Annie and I are continually amazed at all the hospitals, schools, orphanages, universities, homeless shelters, rehabilitation centers, and other humanitarian organizations that are founded in the name of Jesus. We also witness the great work other religions do in the name of agape.

In the end, I prefer being called a Follower rather than an Episcopalian or a Christian. This term constantly reminds me how important Jesus has been to me and my life's journey. I want to follow his example until the end of my life.

When theism died, so did the possibility that anything happens after this life. The Old Testament says it best: "You are dust and to dust you shall return" (Gen. 3:19). With all the scientific discoveries in the last hundred years, the concept of reincarnation or people coming back from the dead or clairvoyants or a heart-shaped soul flitting off to heaven seems highly unlikely to me. If others want to believe any of those things, that's fine, but I believe that dead means dead.

As he faced his own death from cancer, Steve Jobs, CEO of Apple, shared these wise words: "No one wants to die. Even people who want to go to heaven don't want to die to get there. And yet death is the destination we all share. No one has ever escaped it. And that is as it should be, because Death is the single best invention of Life. It is Life's change agent. It clears out the old and makes way for the new."[5]

If we use this way of thinking, perhaps it's good that the institutional church is dying—let's clear away the old, limiting beliefs of institutionalized religion and make way for heaven on earth. There is only one way to do that: live life every day to its fullest. Any day could be our last, so it's up to us to make each day count. Here is the formula I use:

- Eat at least three nutritious meals; exercise to keep your bones strong, your muscles firm, your balance steady, and your heart pumping; and get a good night's sleep of seven to nine hours. As Paul says, "Your body is a temple of the Holy Spirit within you" (I Cor. 6:19).

- Stimulate your mind by attending lectures, watching good movies (some bad ones are okay too), or listening to provocative lectures.

- Spend quiet time reading, reflecting, and reminding yourself what you need to do each day for you, your fellow human beings, and Creation.

- Smile a lot and laugh hard at good stories, jokes, and yourself.

- Continually feed and nurture your relationships with your significant other, your families, and your friends. Make contact with others every day, whether in person, by phone, or online.

- Treat every human being as divinity and repair all broken relationships immediately, remembering that being unforgiving is counterproductive.

- ◆ View your glass as half full, and use the resurrection metaphor to make your Bad Fridays into Easters.

- ◆ Practice agape, volunteer to help those in need, and take action to carry out Jesus's message.

I'll bet you could add many items to this list, but the most important tool for living a full life is agape. No matter what your beliefs are, you can use agape to guide every action of your lives. This is my idea of heaven on earth.

So what are you waiting for? Stop cramming and start living!

PEACE LOVE JOY HOPE

---

*Live each day as if it's your last and
one of these days you'll be right!*
—Fred Allen

Afterword

I have introduced a myriad of ideas in this book, but I have not expanded on any of them. I could have included many other life-changing events from my faith journey, but I wanted to write a book that gave my readers permission to think outside the "walls" of the institutional church, whose walls can be rather limited. I wanted to introduce many subjects, hoping that readers find something that might help them in their faith journey, if they even have one. Although at times my thinking process has gotten me in trouble, the bottom line is that I ended up at about the same place as the church: Jesus is my Christ, and my job in life is to agape.

However, we can continue the conversation if you go to my website (http://peacelovejoyhope.com) and click on my blog, "What Bil Is Saying." There you will have an opportunity to ask questions, make comments, and even share feelings—good or not so good. I invite you to either join the conversation or start one of you own.

Notes

Chapter 1

1. David Keighley, "Leaving Home," quoted in John Shelby Spong, "Iowa's Vote—National and International Scandals," A New Christianity for a New World, January 9, 2008, http://johnshelbyspong .com/2008/01/09/iowas-vote-national-and-international-scandals/.

Chapter 2

1. Paul Tillich, *The Ground of Being: Neglected Essays of Paul Tillich*, ed. Robert M. Price (n.p., Mindvendor, 2015), 133.

2. *The Oxford Dictionary of the Christian Church*, s.v. "theism."

3. "The Holy Eucharist: Rite I," in *The Book of Common Prayer* (New York: Church Publishing, 2007), 337, http://www .episcopalchurch.org/files/book_of_common_prayer.pdf.

4. "The Holy Eucharist: Rite II," in *The Book of Common Prayer*, 364.

5. Ibid.

6. Paul Alan Laughlin, "Prayer without Seeking: Toward a Truly Mystical Lord's Prayer," *Fourth R*, November–December 2009, 21, http://laughlinonline.net/PrayPt2.pdf.

7. Joan Chittister, *The Monastic Way*, February 17, 2014.

Chapter 3

1. "The Gospel of the Birth of Mary," in *The Lost Books of the Bible*, ed. Rutherford H. Platt, Jr. (New York: Testament Books/Random House, 1979).

2. "Thomas's Gospel of the Infancy of Jesus Christ," in *The Lost Books of the Bible*, 61.

3. Kersey Graves, *The World's Sixteen Crucified Saviors: Christianity before Christ* (New York: Cosimo Classics, 2007). First published 1875.

4. Bart D. Ehrman, *How Jesus Became God: The Exaltation of a Jewish Preacher from Galilee* (San Francisco: HarperOne, 2014) and Bart D. Ehrman, *How Jesus Became God*, DVD, The Great Courses, 4 discs (Chantilly, VA: The Teaching Company, 2014).

Chapter 4

1. Robert W. Funk and the Jesus Seminar, *The Gospel of Jesus: According to the Jesus Seminar* (Farmington, MN: Polebridge Press, 1999).

Chapter 5

1. Marianne Thamm, "Amy Biehl and Her Killers' Gift to South Africa—the Enduring Power of Restorative Justice," *Daily Maverick*, July 29, 2015.

2. Gregg Easterbrook, *Beside Still Waters: Searching for Meaning in an Age of Doubt* (New York: William Morrow, 1998), 313.

3. Ibid., 316–17.

4. Kurt Streeter, "At 93, Rabbi Leonard Beerman Still Stirs Passions with Pacifist Views," *Los Angeles Times*, November 26, 2014.

5. David Von Drehle, "How Do You Forgive a Murder?" *Time*, November 23, 2015.

6. Joseph Fletcher, *Situation Ethics: The New Morality* (Louisville, KY: Westminster John Knox Press, 1966).

7. Ibid., 165.

8. Martin Luther King, Jr., *The Radical King*, ed. Cornel West (Boston: Beacon Press, 2015), 175.

Chapter 6

1. Rachel Held Evans, *Searching for Sunday: Loving, Leaving, and Finding the Church* (Nashville: Nelson Books, 2015), xiii–xiv.

2. Ibid., xiv.

3. Paul Nixon, "The Progressive Alternative Church," chap. 8 in *We Refused to Lead a Dying Church! Churches That Came Back against All Odds* (Cleveland: Pilgrim Press, 2012).

4. Nixon, "The Reborn Church," chap. 3 in *We Refused to Lead a Dying Church.*

5. Nixon, "The Community Center Church," chap. 12 in *We Refused to Lead a Dying Church.*

6. Nixon, "The Reimagined Church," chap. 15 in *We Refused to Lead a Dying Church.*

7. Barry E. Blood, Sr., *Giving Voice to the Silent Pulpit: A Layman Explores the Differences between Popular and Academic Christianity* (Eugene, OR: Resource Publications, 2011), 59.

Chapter 7

1. John Shelby Spong, "Charting a New Reformation, Part I—The Background," A New Christianity for a New World, December 3, 2015, http://johnshelbyspong.com/2015/12/03/charting-a-new-reformation-part-i-the-background/.

2. Ibid.

3. John Shelby Spong, *Why Christianity Must Change or Die: A Bishop Speaks to Believers in Exile—A New Reformation of the Church's Faith and Practice* (San Francisco: Harper, 1998), 183.

4. Ibid., 198.

5. Steve Jobs, commencement address, Stanford University, June 12, 2005, http://news.stanford.edu/2005/06/14/jobs-061505/.

Additional Resources

Blood, Barry E., Sr., *Giving Voice to the Silent Pulpit: A Layman Explores the Differences between Popular and Academic Christianity.* Eugene, OR: Resource Publications, 2011.

Charlesworth, James. *The Historical Jesus: An Essential Guide.* Nashville: Abingdon Press, 2008.

Ehrman, Bart D. *How Jesus Became God: The Exaltation of a Jewish Preacher from Galilee.* San Francisco: HarperOne, 2014.

Evans, Rachel Held. *Searching for Sunday: Loving, Leaving, and Finding the Church.* Nashville: Nelson Books, 2015.

Funk, Robert W. *A Credible Jesus: Fragments of a Vision.* Farmington, MN: Polebridge Press, 2002.

Funk, Robert W., and the Jesus Seminar. *The Gospel of Jesus: According to the Jesus Seminar.* Farmington, MN: Polebridge Press, 1999.

Galston, David. *Embracing the Human Jesus: A Wisdom Path for Contemporary Christianity.* Farmington, MN: Polebridge Press, 2012.

Graves, Kersey. *The World's Sixteen Crucified Saviors: Christianity before Christ.* New York: Cosimo Classics, 2007. First published 1875.

Hagenston, Richard. *Fabricating Faith: How Christianity Became a Religion Jesus Would Have Rejected.* Farmington, MN: Polebridge Press, 2014.

Miller, Robert J., ed. *The Complete Gospels.* 4th ed. Farmington, MN: Polebridge Press, 2010.

Nixon, Paul. *We Refused to Lead a Dying Church! Churches That Came Back against All Odds*. Cleveland: Pilgrim Press, 2012.

Scott, Bernard Brandon, ed. *Finding the Historical Jesus: Rules of Evidence*. Farmington, MN: Polebridge Press, 2008.

Spong, John Shelby. *Why Christianity Must Change or Die: A Bishop Speaks to Believers in Exile—A New Reformation of the Church's Faith and Practice*. San Francisco: Harper, 1998.

Tillich, Paul. *Systematic Theology*. Vol. I. Chicago: University of Chicago Press, 1973.

Index

P

pain, 58

Paul, xi, 33–34

    authentic works of, 68

    historical knowledge of, 68–69

    information about Jesus from, 48

    and Jesus as Messiah, 62–63

    lack of reference to nativity story, 56

    letters attributed to, 68

    writings about Jesus by, 67–70

People Helpers, Inc., 20

Peter, Gospel of, 74

Peter, walking on water miracle and, 36

Pharisees, 82, 83, 84

philia, 92

Philip, Gospel of, 72

Philippians 2:12, 70

Philip (Roman ruler), 78

Pietà (Michelangelo), 35

Pontius Pilate, 78

prayer, 37–38, 117, 120

    Jesus Prayer, 38–39, 108

    Lord's Prayer, 38, 107–109

"Prayers of the People, The," 94

Prejean, Sister Helen, 93

programs, church, 103

progressive churches, 109–111, 117

purgatory, 120

Q

Quetzalcoatl, 54–55

Quirinius of Rome, 55

R

Radical King, The, 99

"reconversion" experience, 5–6

rector, xv

reincarnation, 121

religions, 27, 34

remarriage, 96

resurrection, 120

    in gospels, 63

    of Jesus look-alikes, 53, 55

resurrection (*continued*)

    as metaphor, 57–60

Revelation, 33, 52, 120

Roman Catholic Church, 10, 42, 64

Roman Empire, 56, 57, 77–78

Romans 1:4, 62

Romans 6:9, 62

S

Samaritans, 83–84, 93

Satan, 34

Saul, 33, 68

    See also Paul

Savior, Gospel of the, 74

Schutter, Father Tom, xiii, 42

Sea of Galilee, 81

Searching for Sunday (Evans), 106–107

Second Coming, 33, 48, 100, 120

Secret Book of James, 71

seminaries

    author's time in, 7–10

    making changes in, 104–105

    progressive, 117

    sharing academic ideas learned in, 112–113

separation, 30

seraphim, 34

serving others, 90

sin, 30, 33–34

Situation Ethics, 95–97

Situation Ethics (Fletcher), 95, 96

Sitz im leben, 77

Spirit of Agape, 29

Spong, John S., 24, 38, 43, 115–117

St. Mattress (St. Sack's), xv, 21, 22

St. Michael's, Philadelphia, 4

St. Paul. *See* Paul

storge, 92

suffering, 58

Sunday school theology, xv, 3–4, 7–8

symbolism, 41

synoptic gospels, 35, 88

    See also individual gospels

About the Author

The Reverend Dr. William H. Aulenbach served as an Episcopal clergyman, pastor, and teacher for several decades. After receiving his master's of theology from the Church Divinity School of the Pacific in Berkeley, California, he spent fifteen years in the Diocese of Hawaii, where he was a rector, a vicar to a Hawaiian congregation, a youth minister to more than 2,500 teenagers, and the founder of a drug clinic, coffeehouse, and runaway shelter. He then returned to California, where worked in the Diocese of Los Angeles for thirty years.

He is the author of several books, including *What's Love Got to Do with It?* and *How to Get to Heaven Without Going to Church.*

He and his wife, Anne, have three daughters and live in Southern California.

For more information about Bil and his books or to sign up to receive his thought-provoking blog, visit his website, Peace Love Joy Hope (peacelovejoyhope.com). You can also connect with Fr. Bil through Facebook (www.facebook.com/WilliamAulenbach/) and LinkedIn (www.linkedin.com/in/bilaulenbach/).